# FAMILY

## STAGES OF PARENTING

| | | ENTRY LEVEL | ADVANCED LEVEL |
|---|---|---|---|
| SESSION 1 | **Getting Acquainted** | The Big Day<br>Matthew 1:18–25 | |
| SESSION 2 | **It's a Boy!** | Humble Beginnings<br>Luke 2:1–7 | The Pain and the Hope<br>Romans 8:18–27 |
| SESSION 3 | **Diaper Days** | Presented at<br>the Temple<br>Luke 2:21–40 | Parental Model<br>1 Thess. 2:6b–12 |
| SESSION 4 | **He Got That From You** | Growing Pains<br>Luke 2:41–52 | Honor Roll<br>Ephesians 6:1–9 |
| SESSION 5 | **Parents in Pain** | Fracas in the Family<br>Luke 15:11–32 | Painful Times<br>2 Corinthians 1:23–2:4 |
| SESSION 6 | **Parental Expectations** | A Mother's Request<br>Matthew 20:20–28 | God's Expectations<br>Colossians 3:1–17 |
| SESSION 7 | **Family of God** | All in the Family<br>Mark 3:20–21,<br>31–35 | Forever Family<br>Ephesians 2:11–22 |

**Serendipity House / P.O. Box 1012 / Littleton, CO 80160**

TOLL FREE 1-800-525-9563 / www.serendipityhouse.com

00  01  02 / **101 series** • **CHG** / 5  4

**PROJECT ENGINEER:**
Lyman Coleman

**WRITING TEAM:**
Richard Peace, Lyman Coleman, Matthew Lockhart, Andrew Sloan, Cathy Tardif

**PRODUCTION TEAM:**
Christopher Werner, Sharon Penington, Erika Tiepel

**COVER PHOTO:**
© Barbara Peacock / FPG International LLC.

---

### CORE VALUES

| | |
|---|---|
| **Community:** | The purpose of this curriculum is to build community within the body of believers around Jesus Christ. |
| **Group Process:** | To build community, the curriculum must be designed to take a group through a step-by-step process of sharing your story with one another. |
| **Interactive Bible Study:** | To share your "story," the approach to Scripture in the curriculum needs to be open-ended and right brain—to "level the playing field" and encourage everyone to share. |
| **Developmental Stages:** | To provide a healthy program in the life cycle of a group, the curriculum needs to offer courses on three levels of commitment: (1) Beginner Stage—low-level entry, high structure, to level the playing field; (2) Growth Stage—deeper Bible study, flexible structure, to encourage group accountability; (3) Discipleship Stage—in-depth Bible study, open structure, to move the group into high gear. |
| **Target Audiences:** | To build community throughout the culture of the church, the curriculum needs to be flexible, adaptable and transferable into the structure of the average church. |

---

### ACKNOWLEDGMENTS

To Zondervan Bible Publishers
for permission to use
the NIV text,
*The Holy Bible, New International Bible Society.*
© 1973, 1978, 1984 by International Bible Society.
Used by permission of Zondervan Bible Publishers.

# Questions and Answers

**PURPOSE**

1. **What is the purpose of this group?**

   In a nutshell, the purpose is to get acquainted and to double the size of the group.

**STAGE**

2. **What stage in the life cycle of a small group is this course designed for?**

   This 101 course is designed for the first stage in the three-stage life cycle of a small group. (See diagram below.) For a full explanation of the three-stage life cycle, see the center section.

**GOALS**

3. **What is the purpose of stage one in the life cycle?**

   The focus in this first stage is primarily on Group Building.

**GROUP BUILDING**

4. **How does this course develop Group Building?**

   Take a look at the illustration of the baseball diamond on page M5 in the center section. In the process of using this course, you will go around the four bases.

**BIBLE STUDY**

5. **What is the approach to Bible Study in this course?**

   As shown on page M4 of the center section, there are two tracks in this book. Option 1 is based on stories in the Bible. Option 2 is based on teaching passages in the Bible.

**THREE-STAGE LIFE CYCLE OF A GROUP**

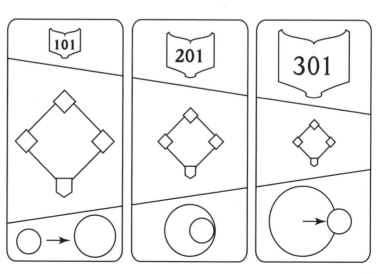

**6. Which option of Bible Study is best for our group?**

Option 1 is the best choice for people not familiar with the Bible, as well as for groups who are not familiar with each other. Option 2 is the best choice for groups who are familiar with the Bible *and* with one another. (However, whenever you have new people come to a meeting, we recommend you switch to Option 1 for that Bible Study.)

**7. Can we choose both options?**

Yes, depending upon your time schedule. Here's how to decide:

| STUDY | APPROXIMATE COMPLETION TIME |
| --- | --- |
| Option 1 only | 60–90 minutes |
| Option 2 only | 60–90 minutes |
| Options 1 and 2 | 90–120 minutes |

**8. What if we want to do both Options 1 and 2 but don't have time at the session?**

You can spend two weeks on a unit—Option 1 (the Gospel Study or Story Passage) the first week and Option 2 (the Epistle Study) the next. Session 1 has only one Bible Study—so you would end up with 13 weeks if you followed this plan.

**9. What if you don't know anything about the Bible?**

No problem. Option 1 is based on a parable or story that stands on its own—to discuss as though you are hearing it for the first time. Option 2 comes complete with reference notes—to help you understand the context of the Bible passage and any difficult words that need to be defined.

## THE FEARLESS FOURSOME

If you have more than seven people at a meeting, Serendipity recommends you divide into groups of 4 for the Bible Study. Count off around the group: "one, two, one, two, etc."—and have the "ones" move quickly to another room for the Bible Study. Ask one person to be the leader and follow the directions for the Bible Study time. After 30 minutes, the Group Leader will call "Time" and ask all groups to come together for the Caring Time.

**MISSION /
MULTIPLICATION**

**10. What is the mission of a 101 group?**

Turn to page M5 of the center section. This course is designed for groups in the Birth stage—which means that your mission is to increase the size of the group by filling the "empty chair."

**THE EMPTY
CHAIR**

**11. How do we fill the empty chair?**

Pull up an empty chair during the group's prayer time and ask God to bring a new person to the group to fill it.

**GROUND
RULES**

**12. What are the ground rules for the group?** It's very important that your group discuss these rules—preferably as part of the first session. (Check those that you agree upon.)

❐ PRIORITY: While you are in the course, you give the group meetings priority.

❐ PARTICIPATION: Everyone participates and no one dominates.

❐ RESPECT: Everyone is given the right to their own opinion and all questions are encouraged and respected.

❐ CONFIDENTIALITY: Anything that is said in the meeting is never repeated outside the meeting.

❐ EMPTY CHAIR: The group stays open to new people at every meeting.

❐ SUPPORT: Permission is given to call upon each other in time of need—even in the middle of the night.

❐ ADVICE GIVING: Unsolicited advice is not allowed.

❐ MISSION: We agree to do everything in our power to start a new group as our mission (see center section).

**ISSUES**

**13.** As a group, you may want to address the following:

• The time and place this group is going to meet
• Responsibility for refreshments
• Child care

# Getting Acquainted

**3-PART AGENDA**

**ICE-BREAKER**
15 Minutes

**BIBLE STUDY**
30 Minutes

**CARING TIME**
15–45 Minutes

It seems that America has rediscovered the family. There is a renewed interest in maintaining the family as an integral part of our society. From the president on down there are calls to improve "the quality of family life." Some voices call for government-funded day care, while others call for a return to "traditional family values."

The reality is that today's families are anything but traditional. Now, in addition to two-parent families, there are large numbers of single-parent homes and blended families (which usually result from divorce and remarriage). With nontraditional families come nontraditional problems.

> **LEADER: Be sure to read the "Questions and Answers" on pages 3–5. Take some time during this first session to have the group go over the ground rules on page 5. At the beginning of the Caring Time have your group look at pages M1–M3 in the center section of this book.**

For example, one of the biggest problems and concerns in female-headed, single-parent homes is not necessarily the lack of a male image, but the lack of a male income. And blended families often experience awkward adjustment periods when trying to become "one" family.

A Harris poll of 3,000 families found that:

- Parents' greatest concerns are drugs, alcohol, sexual promiscuity and pregnancy.
- 86% of all parents expect their children will go to college.
- About 20% of families express dissatisfaction with family life, primarily due to financial burdens.

Other information:

- Studies show that first-time parents often romanticize parenthood.
- Fewer than 10% of American families have both a male breadwinner and a mother at home tending full-time to the family.

- Three-fifths of the mothers with children under the age of 5 have jobs outside the house.

But despite major changes, the American family is still alive and well. Parents still love their children deeply. Parents still care about how their children turn out. And most couples feel their marriage is worth the time and effort.

In the studies which follow, we will see some of what the Bible has to say concerning the family. First, we will look back at the beginnings of our family. We'll consider various stages of parenting. Then, we will examine the issues of parental pain and expectations, and what it means to be part of the larger family of God.

Every session has three parts: (1) **Ice-Breaker**—to break the ice and introduce the topic, (2) **Bible Study**—to share your life through a passage of Scripture, and (3) **Caring Time**—to share prayer concerns and pray for one another.

# Ice-Breaker / 15 Minutes

**All in the Family.** What is your current family like? Help your small group become familiar with your family. First, share briefly about the members of your family—including their names and the ages of your children. Then, select a movie or a comic strip which best describes your family. Tell your group what you have chosen and feel free to explain your selection.

IF MY FAMILY WERE A MOVIE, IT WOULD BE:

❐ Nightmare on Elm Street ❐ Parenthood
❐ The Parent Trap ❐ Rambo
❐ It's a Wonderful Life ❐ Father of the Bride
❐ Home Alone ❐ Twister
❐ The Brady Bunch ❐ Star Wars
❐ The Addams Family ❐ Romeo and Juliet

IF MY FAMILY WERE A COMIC STRIP, IT WOULD BE:

❐ Blondie ❐ Calvin and Hobbes
❐ Peanuts ❐ For Better, For Worse
❐ Family Circus ❐ Dennis the Menace
❐ The Far Side ❐ Outland
❐ Hagar the Horrible ❐ B.C.
❐ Andy Capp ❐ Snuffy Smith

In this first session, you will have a chance to compare your family to a story in Scripture. Ask one person to read out loud the Scripture passage below. Then, follow the guided questions that follow. Be sure to save time at the close to discuss the issues in the Caring Time.

# Bible Study / 30 Minutes

## Matthew 1:18–25 / The Big Day

Read Matthew 1:18–25 and discuss your responses to the following questions with your group. Be sure to save time at the close to discuss the issues in the Caring Time.

*¹⁸This is how the birth of Jesus Christ came about: His mother Mary was pledged to be married to Joseph, but before they came together, she was found to be with child through the Holy Spirit. ¹⁹Because Joseph her husband was a righteous man and did not want to expose her to public disgrace, he had in mind to divorce her quietly.*

*²⁰But after he had considered this, an angel of the Lord appeared to him in a dream and said, "Joseph son of David, do not be afraid to take Mary home as your wife, because what is conceived in her is from the Holy Spirit. ²¹She will give birth to a son, and you are to give him the name Jesus, because he will save his people from their sins."*

*²²All this took place to fulfill what the Lord had said through the prophet: ²³"The virgin will be with child and will give birth to a son, and they will call him Immanuel"—which means, "God with us."*

*²⁴When Joseph woke up, he did what the angel of the Lord had commanded him and took Mary home as his wife. ²⁵But he had no union with her until she gave birth to a son. And he gave him the name Jesus.*

1. What was your reaction when you found out you were going to have your first baby?
   ❑ Wonderful!
   ❑ Can we afford this?
   ❑ It's about time.
   ❑ Oh no! Not yet!
   ❑ other:_____

2. Thinking back, how prepared were you to be a parent when you started out?

   ❏ I was fully prepared.     ❏ I knew a little bit.

   ❏ I was basically prepared.     ❏ I was totally unprepared.

3. How did you decide on a name for your firstborn child?

4. If you had been Mary when she found out she was pregnant, what would be the first thing to pop into your mind?

   ❏ No one will believe me, especially Joseph.

   ❏ What will people say?

   ❏ My parents will kick me out!

   ❏ Surely God must know what he's doing.

5. If you had been Joseph, her fiancé, what would be the first thing to come into your mind?

   ❏ There must be some other guy.

   ❏ What will people say?

   ❏ She's never lied to me before—maybe she's telling the truth.

   ❏ Surely God must know what he's doing.

6. What would you have done if you were Mary or Joseph?

   ❏ supported my spouse     ❏ left town fast

   ❏ trusted God for the next step     ❏ other:_____

   ❏ found the best psychiatrist in Bethlehem

7. When Jesus was conceived, he came with a God-given set of expectations—that he would save his people from their sins. What phrase best describes the expectations you had for your first child when you learned that he or she was on the way?

   ❏ Let's plan the presidential campaign.

   ❏ Is it too early to buy a baseball glove?

   ❏ Does anybody know any good modeling agents?

   ❏ Someone better warn Yale and Harvard, so they can start a recruiting war.

   ❏ I just hope my child can survive my parenting.

   ❏ other:_____

8. What motivated you to come to this group?

   ❏ curiosity

   ❏ a friend asked me

   ❏ my spouse made me

   ❏ I had nothing better to do.

   ❏ a nagging suspicion that I'd better work on my family life

   ❏ other:_____

**9.** What are your expectations for this group?
- ❐ to get to know some other parents
- ❐ to relax and forget about the pressures of family for a while
- ❐ to see what the Bible has to say about family
- ❐ to explore healthier ways to relate to each other in our family
- ❐ to "compare notes" with other parents
- ❐ to have a positive experience sharing this course with my spouse
- ❐ other:_____

**10.** How do you feel about opening up and sharing with this group?
- ❐ nervous
- ❐ okay, but ...
- ❐ concerned about what my spouse might say
- ❐ How far is this going to go?
- ❐ I'm not the sharing type.

**11.** If you are going to belong to this group, what is one thing you want understood?
- ❐ I can "pass" if I want to.
- ❐ Anything that is said stays in this room.
- ❐ I'm not the gushy type.
- ❐ Please don't push me.

# Caring Time / 15–45 Minutes

The most important time in every meeting is this—the Caring Time—where you take time to share prayer requests and pray for one another. To make sure this time is not neglected, you need to set a minimum time that you will devote to prayer requests and prayer and count backward from the closing time by this amount. For instance, if you are going to close at 9 p.m., and you are going to devote 30 minutes to prayer requests and prayer, you need to ask a timekeeper to call "time" at 8:30 and move to prayer requests. Start out by asking everyone to answer this question:

*"How can we help you in prayer this week?"*

Then, move into prayer. If you have not prayed out loud before, finish these sentences:

*"Hello, God, this is ... (first name). I want to thank you for ..."*

Be sure to pray for the "empty chair" (see page M5 in the center section). Think about who you could invite to join you as the group begins this study.

**LEADER:** Ask the group, "Who are you going to invite for next week?"

**GROUP DIRECTORY**

P.S.
At the close, pass around your books and have everyone sign the Group Directory inside the front cover.

# SESSION

# 2

# It's a Boy!

**3-PART AGENDA**

**ICE-BREAKER**
15 Minutes

**BIBLE STUDY**
30 Minutes

**CARING TIME**
15–45 Minutes

Each stage of parenting is full of pleasures as well as intimidating challenges. That is certainly true with the birth process itself. There is no other experience quite like the experience of giving birth. For most mothers (no matter how difficult their labor or how long their delivery), it is all soon forgotten when they see their newborn child. Fathers also experience great joy when they see the one they helped to create for the first time. With the opportunity that most fathers have today of being present in the delivery room, they are able to see their child the moment he or she emerges into the world.

With the pleasures come the challenges. The challenges of the birth stage mainly concern adjustment. Parents have to adjust to new financial stresses (Can we afford this child?) and to the new family dynamic (It's no longer just the two of us!). In this session, you will have the chance to share both the pleasures and the challenges of when you first became a parent.

**LEADER: If there are new people in this session, review the ground rules for this group on page 5. Have the group look at page M4 in the center section and decide which Bible Study option to use— light or heavy. If you have more than seven people, see the box about the "Fearless Foursome" on page 4.**

Starting with this session, there are two options for the Bible Study. Option 1— for beginner groups— starts out with a familiar passage from Luke's Gospel on the birth of Jesus. We will discover some of the challenges Jesus' parents faced at that time. Option 2—for deeper groups—is a teaching passage from Paul's letter to the Romans. In that study, we will see the relationship between pleasures and challenges, both in our childbirth as well as in what God is "bringing to birth" in our world.

To get started, take a few minutes and share your ideas about what, in your opinion, is an ideal family. Answer the questions in the following ice-breaker. Be sure to save plenty of time in this session for the Caring Time—to share your concerns and pray for one another. This is what this course is all about.

# Ice-Breaker / 15 Minutes

1. What number of children do you think is the ideal size for a family?
   - ❐ 0 children
   - ❐ 1 child
   - ❐ 2–3 children
   - ❐ 4 children
   - ❐ 5–6 children
   - ❐ 7–9 children
   - ❐ cheaper by the dozen

2. Which three of the following characteristics do you think are most important for parents to possess? Why?
   - ___ dedication
   - ___ patience
   - ___ gentleness
   - ___ authority
   - ___ kindness
   - ___ unselfishness
   - ___ sense of humor
   - ___ flexibility
   - ___ firmness
   - ___ perseverance
   - ___ perfection
   - ___ wisdom
   - ___ stamina
   - ___ faith
   - ___ love
   - ___ sympathy

# Bible Study / 30 Minutes

## Option 1 / Gospel Study

## Luke 2:1–7 / Humble Beginnings

This version of Christ's birth, from Luke's Gospel, shows Luke's characteristic interest in historical detail. Read Luke 2:1–7 and discuss your responses to the following questions with your group.

**2** *In those days Caesar Augustus issued a decree that a census should be taken of the entire Roman world. ²(This was the first census that took place while Quirinius was governor of Syria.) ³And everyone went to his own town to register.*

*⁴So Joseph also went up from the town of Nazareth in Galilee to Judea, to Bethlehem the town of David, because he belonged to the house and line of David. ⁵He went there to register with Mary, who was pledged to be married to him and was expecting a child. ⁶While they were there, the time came for the baby to be born, ⁷and she gave birth to her firstborn, a son. She wrapped him in cloths and placed him in a manger, because there was no room for them in the inn.*

**1.** If you had been a reporter for *The Bethlehem Herald* at this time, interviewing the parents about this unusual birth, what would have been the first question you asked?
❐ How did Mary ever hold up during that long trip?
❐ Why didn't you call ahead for reservations?
❐ How do you feel about the innkeeper putting you out here?
❐ What are your hopes and fears regarding the future?

**2.** Pregnant. Broke. Homeless. What chance would you give Joseph and Mary of being good parents?
❐ none
❐ uphill all the way
❐ fifty-fifty
❐ a great way to begin

**3.** How would their "humble" beginnings prepare them for parenting?
❐ It gave them a dose of the real world.
❐ It caused them to grow up fast.
❐ It caused them to depend upon God.
❐ It showed them that struggle is the best teacher.

**4.** How would you compare your start as a family to Mary and Joseph's?
❐ We were also very young.
❐ We didn't have much either.
❐ We were also under much stress.
❐ At least we had a place to stay.
❐ Our start was much easier.

**5.** What caused most of the strain early in your marriage relationship?
❐ financial struggles
❐ vocational struggles
❐ relational struggles—between us
❐ relational struggles—with others
❐ a pregnancy early in our marriage

**6.** What is the major source of stress in your family now?
| | |
|---|---|
| ❐ employment issues | ❐ religion |
| ❐ money | ❐ illness |
| ❐ alcohol / drugs | ❐ parent-child conflict |
| ❐ neighbors | ❐ relatives / in-laws |
| ❐ workaholism | ❐ marital conflict |
| ❐ being a blended family | ❐ other:_____ |

7. If you could go back to the early days in your family life, would you?
   ❐ It was sure easier then than it is now.
   ❐ I'm glad we started out that way, but I would not go back.
   ❐ In some ways "yes" and in other ways "no."
   ❐ No way!
   ❐ other:_____

8. What did you learn from the early days in your family life that you would like to pass on to your children?
   ❐ Keep a sense of humor.
   ❐ Struggles will deepen your relationship.
   ❐ God didn't promise an easy path, but he promised his presence.
   ❐ I would never give my kids advice.
   ❐ other: _____

## Option 2 / Epistle Study

## Romans 8:18–27 / The Pain and the Hope

In this passage, Paul compares the sufferings of the present time with the pain of childbirth, because it is pain that is full of hope for what is to come. Read Romans 8:18–27 and discuss the questions which follow with your group. The reference notes on pages 17–18 will help you better understand the passage.

*18I consider that our present sufferings are not worth comparing with the glory that will be revealed in us. 19The creation waits in eager expectation for the sons of God to be revealed. 20For the creation was subjected to frustration, not by its own choice, but by the will of the one who subjected it, in hope 21that the creation itself will be liberated from its bondage to decay and brought into the glorious freedom of the children of God.*

*22We know that the whole creation has been groaning as in the pains of childbirth right up to the present time. 23Not only so, but we ourselves, who have the firstfruits of the Spirit, groan inwardly as we wait eagerly for our adoption as sons, the redemption of our bodies. 24For in this hope we were saved. But hope that is seen is no hope at all. Who hopes for what he already has? 25But if we hope for what we do not yet have, we wait for it patiently.*

*26In the same way, the Spirit helps us in our weakness. We do not know what we ought to pray for, but the Spirit himself intercedes for us with groans that words cannot express. 27And he who searches our hearts knows the mind of the Spirit, because the Spirit intercedes for the saints in accordance with God's will.*

1. In the birth of your first child, what were the most difficult "pains" you had to suffer?
   ❏ giving up our freedom to go where we wanted when we wanted
   ❏ the financial drain
   ❏ the physical pain
   ❏ giving up the exclusive attention of my spouse
   ❏ the changes in our sexual life
   ❏ the anxiety of raising a child in this world
   ❏ the fear of a child with physical or mental abnormalities

2. When you were approaching the birth of your first child, what were the relative roles of hope and pain in the way you looked at your situation?

3. What is the difference between the hope of a Christian and wishful thinking?

4. What does the Holy Spirit do for us when we do not know how to pray (vv. 26–27)?

5. When was the last time you did not know how to pray, particularly for your family, and the Holy Spirit helped you?

6. What are your "present sufferings" as a parent?

7. What comfort do you draw from this passage for your situation as a parent?

# Caring Time / 15–45 Minutes

Take time at the close to share any personal prayer requests. Answer the question:

*"How can we help you in prayer this week?"*

**LEADER:**
Ask the group, "Who are you going to invite for next week?"

Then go around and let each person pray for the person on their right. Finish this sentence:

*"Dear God, I want to speak to you about my friend _____."*

During your prayer time, remember to pray for the empty chair and for the growth of your group.

**8:18–27** In this passage, Paul focuses on the fact that Christians are the heirs of God. It is this idea of inheritance that leads to the theme of verses 18–27: the hope which people have who are indwelt by the Spirit of God. Paul first discusses what it is that is hoped for (vv. 18–19,21,23b). He then sets this hope of glory over against the pain of the present (vv. 20,22,23–25). He ends by pointing out that the Holy Spirit "groans" alongside those who groan (due to their suffering).

**8:18** *sufferings / glory.* Paul defines the basic contrast that will be the subject of verses 18–27. His point: one's future glory (inheritance) vastly outweighs one's present distress (sufferings).

*present sufferings.* The persecution that Christians will experience in the time between Jesus' first coming and his future return. These are real; not pleasant, but slight in comparison with the glory ahead.

**8:19–21** The fate of humanity and of the universe are intertwined. Just as through Adam's sin, creation also fell (Gen. 3:17); so too through the redemption of the sons of Adam, creation will itself be restored (Rev. 22:3).

**8:19** *eager expectation.* The image is of a person with excited anticipation scanning the horizon for the first sign of the coming dawn of glory.

*for the sons of God to be revealed.* Christians are indeed sons and daughters of God here and now in this life. What Paul refers to here is the fact that they are, as it were, incognito. It will only be at the Second Coming that it is revealed for all to see who are, in fact, the children of God.

**8:20** *the creation.* The whole of the nonhuman world, both living and inanimate.

*was subjected.* The verb tense indicates a single past action (see Gen. 3:17–19).

*frustration.* The inability of creation to achieve the goal for which it was created—that of glorifying God—because the key actor in this drama of praise (humankind) has fallen.

*in hope.* There was divine judgment at the Fall, but this was not without hope. One day, it was said, the woman's offspring would crush the serpent's head (Gen. 3:15).

**8:21 *will be liberated.*** Creation will be freed from its frustrating bondage at the time of the Second Coming when the children of God are also freed from the last vestiges of sin.

***bondage to decay.*** All of creation seems to be running down; deterioration and decomposition characterize the created order.

**8:22 *pains of childbirth.*** Such pain is very real, very intense, but also temporary (and the necessary prelude to new life). The image is not of the annihilation of the present universe but of the emergence of a transformed order (Rev. 21:1).

**8:23 *firstfruits.*** Generally this term refers to those early-developing pieces of fruit that were harvested and given to God, but here the idea is of a gift from God to people. The experience by the believer of the work of the Holy Spirit is a pledge that one day God will grant all that he has promised.

***we ... groan inwardly.*** One groans not just because of persecution, but because one is not yet fully redeemed. Believers' bodies are still subject to weakness, pain and death. The believer therefore longs for the suffering to end and for the redemption of the body to be complete.

***we wait eagerly.*** In one sense a Christian is already an adopted child of God, but in another sense they have yet to experience fully their inheritance.

**8:26–27** Human frailty affects even prayer. Sometimes feelings are so deep and so inexpressible that it is the Holy Spirit himself who must pray for an individual. "Prayer is the Divine in us appealing to the Divine above us" (C.H. Dodd).

**8:26 *what ... to pray.*** It is not clear whether this phrase refers to one's inability to know what one ought to pray, or to the problem in knowing how to pray.

**GROUP DIRECTORY**

P.S.
If you have a new person in your group, be sure to add their name to the group directory inside the front cover.

# SESSION 3

# Diaper Days

## 3-PART AGENDA

### ICE-BREAKER
15 Minutes

### BIBLE STUDY
30 Minutes

### CARING TIME
15–45 Minutes

Once a child is born, we as parents have both new pleasures and new challenges. The new pleasures center around seeing our child develop his or her own unique personality. We take delight in a special smile we come to understand. We experience what our child adds to our life.

The new challenges, on the other hand, center around discipline. What can we do to make sure our child grows into a loving, well-adjusted adult who knows how to take a responsible role in our world? One of the first things we need to do in order to meet this challenge is to enable our child to trust us. Child psychologist Erik Erikson tells us that one of the key issues in a child's first year of life is developing trust. Can our child trust us to provide what they need, both physically and emotionally? Can our child trust us to discipline out of love rather than striking out in anger? These are indeed challenges for us as we seek to be good parents.

LEADER: If there are more than seven people at this meeting, divide into groups of 4 for Bible Study. Count off around the group: "one, two, one, two, etc."—and have the "ones" quickly move to another room. When you come back together for the Caring Time, have the group read about their Mission on page M5 of the center section.

This session will help us talk about early childhood and its associated challenges. In the Option 1 Study (from Luke's Gospel), we will examine the presentation of Mary and Joseph's newborn in the temple. We will also examine what similar acts we can do for our children to "present them to the Lord." In the Option 2 Study, we will learn about Paul's parental model in his letter to the Thessalonians. Both studies will provide an opportunity to discuss your early parenting days.

Remember the purpose of the Bible Study is to share your own story. Use this opportunity to deal with some issues in your life.

Now, to get started, share a few fun stories about your kids with the following ice-breaker.

# Ice-Breaker / 15 Minutes

**The Great American Blush Awards.** Imagine your group is in charge of giving an award for the most embarrassing thing a child has done to his or her parents. Instead of an "Emmy" we can call it a "Ruddy." Find out who in your group has had a child do the following. Then vote on which is the most embarrassing. Give that person (or persons) the "Ruddy"!

- ❏ had a child share an embarrassing family incident during the children's sermon
- ❏ had a child report a less-than-flattering remark you made about someone else
- ❏ had an older child dress oddly when company came over
- ❏ as a single parent, had a child propose to your date for you
- ❏ had a child bring out embarrassing hygiene products for company
- ❏ had a child publicly contradict your "little white lie"
- ❏ had a little girl lift her dress during a public function
- ❏ had a child repeat a "four-letter word" they had heard
- ❏ had a little child shout during a quiet moment of worship, "I have to go potty!"
- ❏ other:_____

# Bible Study / 30 Minutes

## Option 1 / Gospel Study

## Luke 2:21–40 / Presented at the Temple

This story (found only in Luke) concerns Jesus' parents as they fulfill one of the religious obligations of new parents. Read Luke 2:21–40 and discuss your responses to the following questions with your group.

*²¹On the eighth day, when it was time to circumcise him, he was named Jesus, the name the angel had given him before he had been conceived.*

*²²When the time of their purification according to the Law of Moses had been completed, Joseph and Mary took him to Jerusalem to present him to the Lord ²³(as it is written in the Law of the Lord, "Every firstborn male is to* be consecrated to the Lord"), ²⁴and to offer a sacrifice in keeping with what is said in the Law of the Lord: "a pair of doves or two young pigeons."

²⁵Now there was a man in Jerusalem called Simeon, who was righteous and devout. He was waiting for the consolation of Israel, and the Holy Spirit was upon him. ²⁶It had been revealed to him by the Holy Spirit that he would not die before he had seen the Lord's Christ. ²⁷Moved by the Spirit, he went into the temple courts. When the parents brought in the child Jesus to do for him what the custom of the Law required, ²⁸Simeon took him in his arms and praised God, saying:

²⁹"Sovereign Lord, as you have promised,
   you now dismiss your servant in peace.
³⁰For my eyes have seen your salvation,
³¹   which you have prepared in the sight of all people,
³²a light for revelation to the Gentiles
   and for glory to your people Israel."

³³The child's father and mother marveled at what was said about him. ³⁴Then Simeon blessed them and said to Mary, his mother: "This child is destined to cause the falling and rising of many in Israel, and to be a sign that will be spoken against, ³⁵so that the thoughts of many hearts will be revealed. And a sword will pierce your own soul too."

³⁶There was also a prophetess, Anna, the daughter of Phanuel, of the tribe of Asher. She was very old; she had lived with her husband seven years after her marriage, ³⁷and then was a widow until she was eighty-four. She never left the temple but worshiped night and day, fasting and praying. ³⁸Coming up to them at that very moment, she gave thanks to God and spoke about the child to all who were looking forward to the redemption of Jerusalem.

³⁹When Joseph and Mary had done everything required by the Law of the Lord, they returned to Galilee to their own town of Nazareth. ⁴⁰And the child grew and became strong; he was filled with wisdom, and the grace of God was upon him.

1. What was the first "out-of-the-house" trip you took with your newborn child?

2. When you took your first newborn out of the house, what reactions did you get from the people you met?
   ❑ "Gee, he/she looks like Mom."
   ❑ "Gee, he/she looks like Dad."
   ❑ lots of silly baby talk
   ❑ lots of child-rearing advice
   ❑ other parents comparing notes with us
   ❑ the classic question—"Is he/she a *good* baby?"

**3.** If you had been Joseph or Mary and experienced the events in this passage, what would have been the first thing you wrote down in your diary for this day?
❒ "Everybody loved him—I was so proud!"
❒ "Old people say such strange things sometimes!"
❒ "I never had so much to thank the Lord for as I do now!"
❒ "I wonder what that man meant about a sword piercing my (Mary's) soul."

**4.** Why were Mary and Joseph so careful to do "everything required by the Law of the Lord" (v. 39)?
❒ They really needed to get out of the house, and this was a good opportunity.
❒ They wanted to look good.
❒ They didn't want to be punished.
❒ They were good Jews—it was their tradition.
❒ They wanted to be extra careful to raise their child right.
❒ other:_____

**5.** Which of the following acts were (are) on your list for doing "everything required" by the Lord?
❒ baptism, christening or dedication
❒ confirmation
❒ taking my child to church
❒ spending lots of time with my child
❒ praying *for* my child
❒ praying *with* my child
❒ disciplining my child
❒ teaching my child about God
❒ providing for my child's physical needs
❒ providing for my child's education
❒ other:_____

**6.** Which of the actions on your list are your top two priorities right now? Which have been the most difficult for you?

**7.** Do you think God has a plan and purpose for your life as a parent like he did for Mary and Joseph?
❒ not at all
❒ in a way
❒ probably—I wish I knew what it was.
❒ definitely, and I'm still discovering it

**8.** We see in this story that, even in their old age, God had a great purpose for Simeon and Anna. What would be the crowning joy for you in your old age?

❏ to see my children's children
❏ to see my family serving God
❏ to strike it rich
❏ to look back on a life full of surprises
❏ to feel I have done God's will
❏ to leave the world a better place
❏ to know I've spent my days walking with the Lord
❏ other:_____

**COMMENT**

Every culture and society has its rituals surrounding a birth. In our culture, we have baby showers before the birth and visits to the hospital after it. The most important tradition for many of us is the day our baby is taken to church for christening, baptism or dedication.

There are two Old Testament rituals in this passage. First is the ritual of presenting oneself for purification following childbirth. For 40 days after giving birth to her son, Mary was forbidden to go to the temple or to participate in any religious service. Afterward, she offered a sacrifice of two birds for her cleansing.

Second is the ritual of the redemption of the firstborn (see Ex. 13:2). In commemoration of the events surrounding the Passover, the firstborn male in every Jewish family was to be set apart for God. Because Mary and Joseph brought Jesus to the temple (as opposed to simply paying the priest), perhaps it was their intention to dedicate Jesus to God. This is similar to Samuel (1 Sam. 1:11,22,28), who was offered to the service of the priests at the Old Testament tabernacle when he was older.

The responses of Simeon and Anna took Mary and Joseph by surprise. Simeon and Anna had waited on God with consistent prayer for him to bring about the promises of the messianic age (Isa. 40:1–11; 49:8–13). With Jesus' presentation at the temple, they knew that their prayers had been answered and that they could die in peace. But their prophetic words raised more questions in the hearts of Mary and Joseph as to who their son really was.

# Option 2 / Epistle Study

## 1 Thessalonians 2:6b–12 / Parental Model

This passage is Paul's recounting of the way he dealt with the Thessalonians when he started the church in their city. Read 1 Thessalonians 2:6b–12 and discuss your responses to the following questions with your group.

*As apostles of Christ we could have been a burden to you, ⁷but we were gentle among you, like a mother caring for her little children. ⁸We loved you so much that we were delighted to share with you not only the gospel of God but our lives as well, because you had become so dear to us. ⁹Surely you remember, brothers, our toil and hardship; we worked night and day in order not to be a burden to anyone while we preached the gospel of God to you.*

*¹⁰You are witnesses, and so is God, of how holy, righteous and blameless we were among you who believed. ¹¹For you know that we dealt with each of you as a father deals with his own children, ¹²encouraging, comforting and urging you to live lives worthy of God, who calls you into his kingdom and glory.*

*"The chances are that you will never be elected president of the country, write the Great American novel, make a million dollars, stop pollution, end racial conflict, or save the world. However valid it may be to work at any of these goals, there is one of higher priority—to be an effective parent."*
*—Landrum R. Bolling*

1. What is your fondest memory of how a parent or grandparent encouraged, comforted or cared for you when you were a child?

2. If you had been one of those who received this letter, what would your reaction have been?
   ❑ I already have a mother, thank you.
   ❑ What a guilt trip!
   ❑ It's nice to have someone care so much.
   ❑ What is he up to?

3. In speaking to the church in Thessalonica, why do you think Paul uses this parental imagery?

4. Who in your life has urged you to live in God's ways?

5. Which of the parental functions that Paul talks about in this letter do you believe you do best as a parent?
   ❑ being gentle
   ❑ sharing my life
   ❑ working night and day for my family
   ❑ modeling Christian behavior
   ❑ encouraging
   ❑ comforting
   ❑ urging my children to live lives worthy of God

24

**6.** Which of the functions in question 5 do you have the hardest time fulfilling?

**7.** What is God saying to you in this passage?

COMMENT Studies have shown that babies need human touch in order to survive (let alone thrive) in life. Paul's letter to the church in Thessalonica states that the same is true for infants in the faith.

Like a mother, Paul states that he gently loves those in the faith. In doing so, he will withhold no care from them. Like a father, Paul will encourage, comfort and urge them in the faith. Undoubtedly, Paul's use of parental imagery (in caring for those in the church) is based on the ways God cares for us. The imagery provides a wonderful model for parents as well.

# Caring Time / 15–45 Minutes

Take some time to share any personal prayer requests and answer the question:

**LEADER:**
Ask the
group, "Who
are you going
to invite for
next week?"

*"What would you like to change
about yourself as a parent?"*

Close with a short time of prayer, remembering the dreams that have been shared. If you would like to pray in silence, say the word "Amen" when you have finished your prayer, so that the next person will know when to start.

## Reference Notes

**2:6 *apostles of Christ.*** This term means one sent with the authority and power of the sender. Paul was divinely commissioned to this task; it was not simply his choice for a religious occupation! Although Paul argued for the right of a religious teacher to expect financial support from the people he teaches (1 Cor. 9:7–14), in both Corinth and Thessalonica he supported himself through his own work and through the gifts of others (see Phil. 4:16; 1 Thess. 2:9).

**2:7 *gentle ... like a mother.*** In contrast to the self-importance of other traveling teachers, Paul compares his love for this church with that of a nursing mother and child. "A mother in nursing her child makes no show of authority and does not stand on any dignity ... she spares no trouble or effort, avoids no care ..." (Calvin).

**2:8 *our lives as well.*** "The true missionary is not someone specialized in the delivery of the message, but someone whose whole being, completely committed to (his) message ... is communicated to his hearers" (Best). One major evidence for the truth of the Gospel message is the love and integrity of the messenger.

**2:10 *holy, righteous and blameless.*** Paul appeals to the Thessalonians' own experience with him regarding his behavior. These terms point to an inner attitude of devotion to God marked by living in obedience to his teachings.

**2:11 *dealt with each of you as a father.*** In the ancient world, the father's role was to see that his children learned how to live as responsible citizens. Paul was not only interested in their spiritual birth (v. 7), but in their growth into maturity. The Greek text of verses 10–12 is a run-on sentence with no verb, so "dealt with" is supplied by the NIV to make sense of the verse.

**2:12 *encouraging, comforting and urging.*** These participles describe Paul's fatherly action with the people. The terms should be read as supporting and amplifying one another rather than as representing distinct functions.

***his kingdom.*** Although the first three Gospels speak of the "kingdom" a great deal, Paul did not use this term very often. It refers both to the present experience of God's reign in our lives (e.g., Rom. 14:17; Col. 1:13), and the future reality believers will one day experience fully (e.g., 1 Cor. 15:50). The latter perspective seems to be in view here.

***glory.*** This is the distinctive characteristic of God that sums up all that he is. While sinful humanity has fallen short of God's glory (Rom. 3:23) by living in a way that flies in the face of his character, the Gospel provides the hope that, through his grace, believers will one day "share in his glory" (Rom. 8:17). Humanity's goal is reached when people take their place with all creation in radiating God's glory without distortion (Rom. 8:18–20).

# He Got That From You

**3-PART AGENDA**

**ICE-BREAKER**
15 Minutes

**BIBLE STUDY**
30 Minutes

**CARING TIME**
15–45 Minutes

Many parents today feel ambivalent about raising children. The demands of a job or career can place excessive stress and pressure on couples (and on single parents, who want to be conscientious in raising their children). In fact, recent studies have shown that most mothers work because they have to—they don't have a choice. About half of these working mothers feel cheated because they are missing out on the best years of their kids' lives. It is little wonder that many young couples have chosen to have few children.

But despite the numerous obstacles in parenting, many families today are thriving. In his book, *Secrets of Strong Families*, Nick Stinnett explains that there are six qualities which are consistently found in strong families:

- COMMITMENT: "They have a sense of being a team."

- APPRECIATION: "These folks help each other feel good about themselves."

- COMMUNICATION: "They spend a lot of time talking and listening."

- TIME TOGETHER: "These families eat, work, play and talk together."

- SPIRITUAL HEALTH: "It is a unifying force that enables them to reach out in love and compassion to others."

- COPING SKILLS: "Some of their coping skills are: seeing something positive in the crises, pulling together, being flexible, drawing on spiritual and communication strengths and getting help from friends and professionals."

**LEADER: If you have a new person at this session, remember to use Option 1 rather than Option 2 for the Bible Study. During the Caring Time, don't forget to keep praying for the empty chair.**

This session focuses on parenting during late childhood. Much of the practical framework for loving, effective parenting comes from the Bible. In Option 1, we will look at a parenting crisis which Mary and Joseph had during Jesus' youth. While Jesus was not really a typical child, we can learn from his parents' actions. We can also glean some parenting wisdom from Paul's teachings in the Ephesians passage in Option 2. Remember, the purpose of the Bible Study is to share your own story. Use this opportunity to deal with issues in your own life.

# Ice-Breaker / 15 Minutes

**Growing Together.** Take a few minutes and share your responses to the following questions.

*1.* When I was growing up, the discipline was likely to come from:
❏ my mother      ❏ my father

*2.* When I was growing up, comfort and sympathy were likely to come from:
❏ my mother      ❏ my father

*3.* When I was growing up, the parent most likely to play with me was:
❏ my mother      ❏ my father

*4.* Which do you think is easier to raise, and why?
❏ a son      ❏ a daughter

*5.* As a parent, which age group do you prefer?
❏ infant      ❏ elementary
❏ toddler      ❏ teenage
❏ preschool

# Bible Study / 30 Minutes

## Option 1 / Gospel Study

## Luke 2:41–52 / Growing Pains

This story is the only one in the Bible about Jesus between his infancy and adulthood. Read Luke 2:41–52 and discuss your responses to the following questions with your group.

*⁴¹Every year his parents went to Jerusalem for the Feast of the Passover. ⁴²When he was twelve years old, they went up to the Feast, according to the custom. ⁴³After the Feast was over, while his parents were returning home, the boy Jesus stayed behind in Jerusalem, but they were unaware of it. ⁴⁴Thinking he was in their company, they traveled on for a day. Then they began looking for him among their relatives and friends. ⁴⁵When they did not find him, they went back to Jerusalem to look for him. ⁴⁶After three days they found him in the temple courts, sitting among the teachers, listening to them and asking them questions. ⁴⁷Everyone who heard him was amazed at his understanding and his answers. ⁴⁸When his parents saw him, they were astonished. His mother said to him, "Son, why have you treated us like this? Your father and I have been anxiously searching for you."*

*⁴⁹"Why were you searching for me?" he asked. "Didn't you know I had to be in my Father's house?" ⁵⁰But they did not understand what he was saying to them.*

*⁵¹Then he went down to Nazareth with them and was obedient to them. But his mother treasured all these things in her heart. ⁵²And Jesus grew in wisdom and stature, and in favor with God and men.*

*"Back when we started out, we had three hard and fast child-rearing principles, but no children. Now, we have three children, but no principles."*
—Anonymous

**1.** What was your first significant time apart from your parents, or a "coming of age" experience as a teenager? What was significant about it?
❏ summer camp
❏ field trip to "the big city"
❏ confirmation class (or a spiritual retreat)
❏ getting a summer job
❏ other:_____

**2.** At age 12, what was the most difficult parenting problem you posed for your parents?
❏ The outbreak of puberty posed innumerable problems.
❏ I raised religious questions my parents couldn't answer.
❏ My peers began to influence me in ways my parents didn't like.
❏ I discovered the opposite sex, and that raised new relational problems.
❏ I began to rebel more, raising new discipline problems.

**3.** What do you think of Jesus' behavior in this story?
❏ He disobeyed his parents.
❏ He was oblivious to his parents.
❏ He put his heavenly Father's concerns over his earthly parents' concerns.
❏ He behaved like a typical 12-year-old.

**4.** What do you think of Mary and Joseph's behavior in this story?
- ❏ They were negligent parents.
- ❏ They didn't know their son very well.
- ❏ They were confused by who Jesus really was.
- ❏ They gave Jesus more freedom than parents can today.
- ❏ They behaved like any good parents would.

**5.** Had you been one of Jesus' parents, how would you have reacted when you discovered Jesus missing?
- ❏ blamed my spouse
- ❏ gone into shock
- ❏ frantically started searching
- ❏ cried and panicked
- ❏ figured he would show up

**6.** If you had been Mary or Joseph, what would you have said to Jesus when you found him three days later?
- ❏ "Don't you ever do that again!"
- ❏ "Why did you run off like that?"
- ❏ "You had us worried sick!"
- ❏ "You're grounded for a month!"
- ❏ "I'm so sorry we forgot you!"
- ❏ "I understand why you're here in the temple."

**7.** How was this incident important to Jesus' development as a preteen?
- ❏ It showed he could take care of himself.
- ❏ It showed he was developing his own faith.
- ❏ It showed he was thinking for himself.
- ❏ He had finished school and could now teach his elders.
- ❏ It showed he knew who he was—the unique Son of God.
- ❏ other:_____

**8.** What do you think you'll really treasure from your children's late childhood years?

**9.** What are (were) your biggest anxieties about parenting children of this age group?

❏ realizing that they're almost teenagers
❏ the increasing influence of peers
❏ school performance
❏ the availability of alcohol and drugs
❏ sexual promiscuity
❏ gangs and violence
❏ the prevalence of child abuse
❏ wondering whether they will still want to be around the family
❏ other:_____

**10.** From this Bible story, what comfort or insight can you find concerning the anxieties you face as a parent?

❏ Even Jesus' parents had to go through stress and challenges.
❏ Even Jesus did things that disturbed his parents.
❏ Developing independence is necessary in growing up.
❏ Parents sometimes misjudge their children.
❏ Children sometimes mature without parents noticing it.
❏ other:_____

**COMMENT**  You might call this a biblical version of *Home Alone!* Jewish pilgrims from outside Jerusalem, such as Jesus' family, generally traveled to and from the Passover celebration in large caravans. Typically, the women and children would be up front while the men and older boys traveled along behind. It would have been easy during the day for Mary and Joseph to each assume that Jesus was with the other parent or with friends.

When they retraced their steps, they found him in a surprising situation. Their little boy was asking some rather penetrating questions of the teachers. One can only imagine Mary and Joseph looking at each other and saying, "Who is that boy?" Despite the special circumstances surrounding Jesus' birth, Mary and Joseph were only beginning to discover the uniqueness of their son.

# Option 2 / Epistle Study

## Ephesians 6:1–9 / Honor Roll

Read Ephesians 6:1–9 and discuss the questions which follow with your group. If you do not understand a word or phrase, check the reference notes on pages 33–35.

**6** Children, obey your parents in the Lord, for this is right. [2]"Honor your father and mother"—which is the first commandment with a promise— [3]"that it may go well with you and that you may enjoy long life on the earth."

[4]Fathers, do not exasperate your children; instead, bring them up in the training and instruction of the Lord.

[5]Slaves, obey your earthly masters with respect and fear, and with sincerity of heart, just as you would obey Christ. [6]Obey them not only to win their favor when their eye is on you, but like slaves of Christ, doing the will of God from your heart. [7]Serve wholeheartedly, as if you were serving the Lord, not men, [8]because you know that the Lord will reward everyone for whatever good he does, whether he is slave or free.

[9]And masters, treat your slaves in the same way. Do not threaten them, since you know that he who is both their Master and yours is in heaven, and there is no favoritism with him.

*1.* Was obeying your parents ever a problem for you? For your children? How do you get your children to mind without losing yours?

*2.* According to Paul, why should children obey their parents?

*3.* What does it mean to "Honor your father and mother" (v. 2; see note on page 34)?

*4.* How can fathers (and mothers) "exasperate" their children?

*5.* How can parents bring up their children "in the training and instruction of the Lord"?

*6.* What are the similarities and dissimilarities in the relationships of slaves to masters and children to parents?

*7.* Would you say the way you discipline your child(ren) is too harsh, too soft, or just right? What would your child(ren) say?

*8.* What one area of your relationship with your child(ren) needs improvement? What might you do to improve this area?

# Leadership Training Supplement

YOU ARE
HERE

| BIRTH | GROWTH | RELEASE |
|-------|--------|---------|

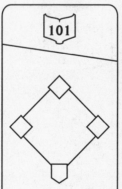

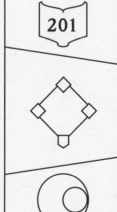

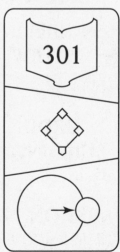

# What is the game plan for your group in the 101 stage?

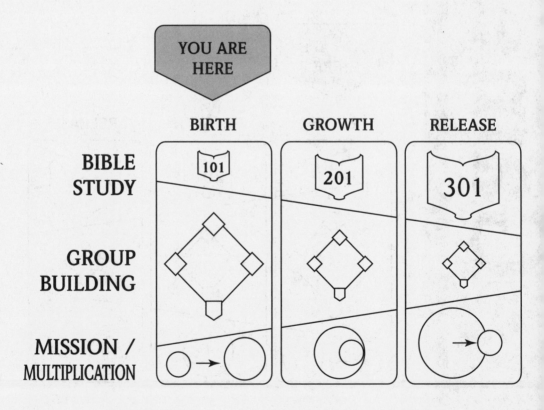

YOU ARE HERE

| | BIRTH | GROWTH | RELEASE |
|---|---|---|---|
| **BIBLE STUDY** | 101 | 201 | 301 |
| **GROUP BUILDING** | | | |
| **MISSION / MULTIPLICATION** | | | |

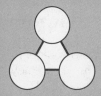

**The 3-Legged Stool**

The three essentials in a healthy small group are Bible Study, Group Building and Mission / Multiplication. You need all three to stay balanced—like a 3-legged stool.
- To focus only on Bible Study will lead to scholasticism.
- To focus only on Group Building will lead to narcissism.
- To focus only on Mission will lead to burnout.

You need a game plan for the life cycle of the group where all three of these elements are present in a mission-driven strategy. In the first stage of the group, here is the game plan:

# Bible Study

**To share your spiritual story through Scripture.**

The greatest gift you can give a group is the gift of your spiritual story—the story of your spiritual beginnings, your spiritual growing pains, struggles, hopes and fears. The Bible Study is designed to help you tell your spiritual story to the group.

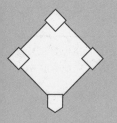

# Group Building

**To become a caring community.**

In the first stage of a group, note how the baseball diamond is larger than the book and the circles. This is because Group Building is the priority in the first stage. Group Building is a four-step process to become a close-knit group. Using the baseball diamond illustration, the goal of Group Building—bonding—is home plate. But to get there you have to go around the bases.

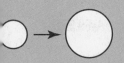

# Mission / Multiplication

**To grow your group numerically and spiritually.**

The mission of your group is the greatest mission anyone can give their life to—to bring new people into a personal relationship with Christ and the fellowship of a Christian community. This purpose will become more prominent in the second and third stages of your group. In this stage, the goal is to invite new people into your group and try to double.

# Bible Study

In the first stage of a group, the Bible Study is where you get to know each other and share your spiritual stories. The Bible Study is designed to give the leader the option of going LIGHT or HEAVY, depending on the background of the people in the group. OPTION 1 is especially designed for beginner groups who do not know a lot about the Bible or each other. OPTION 2 is for groups who are familiar with the Bible and with one another.

## Option 1    Relational Bible Study (Stories)

Designed around a guided questionnaire, the questions move across the Disclosure Scale from "no risk" questions about people in the Bible story to "high risk" questions about your own life and how you would react in that situation. "If you had been in the story ..." or "The person in the story like me is ... " The questions are open-ended—with multiple-choice options and no right or wrong answers. A person with no background knowledge of the Bible may actually have the advantage because the questions are based on first impressions.

| The STORY in Scripture | GUIDED QUESTIONNAIRE 1 2 3 4 5 6 7 8 | My STORY compared |
|---|---|---|

| OPTION 1: Light RELATIONAL BIBLE STUDY | OPTION 2: Heavy INDUCTIVE BIBLE STUDY |
|---|---|
| • Based on Bible stories<br>• Open-ended questions<br>• To share your spiritual story | • Based on Bible teachings<br>• With observation questions<br>• To dig into Scripture |

## Option 2    Inductive Bible Study (Teachings)

For groups who know each other, OPTION 2 gives you the choice to go deeper in Bible Study, with questions about the text on three levels:

- • Observation: What is the text saying?
- • Interpretation: What does it mean?
- • Application: What are you going to do about it?

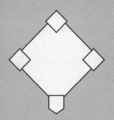

## Group Building

The Baseball Diamond illustrates the four-step sharing process in bonding to become a group: (1) input; (2) feedback; (3) deeper input; and (4) deeper feedback. This process is carefully structured into the seven sessions of this course, as follows:

 **Sharing My Story.** My religious background. My early years and where I am right now in my spiritual journey.

 **Affirming Each Other's Story.** "Thank you for sharing ..." "Your story became a gift to me ..." "Your story helps me to understand where you are coming from ..."

 **Sharing My Needs.** "This is where I'm struggling and hurting. This is where I need to go—what I need to do."

 **Caring for One Another.** "How can we help you in prayer this week?" Ministry occurs as the group members serve one another through the Holy Spirit.

## Mission / Multiplication

To prove that your group is "Mission-Driven," now is the time to start praying for your new "baby"—a new group to be born in the future. This is the MISSION of your group.

The birthing process begins by growing your group to about 10 or 12 people. Here are three suggestions to help your group stay focused on your Mission:

1. **Empty Chair.** Pull up an empty chair at the Caring Time and ask God to fill this chair at the next meeting.

2. **Refrigerator List.** Jot down the names of people you are going to invite and put this list on the refrigerator.

3. **New Member Home.** Move to the home of the newest member—where their friends will feel comfortable when they come to the group. On the next page, some of your questions about bringing new people into your group are answered.

## Q&A

**What if a new person joins the group in the third or fourth session?**

Call the "Option Play" and go back to an OPTION 1 Bible Study that allows this person to "share their story" and get to know the people in the group.

**What do you do when the group gets too large for sharing?**

Take advantage of the three-part agenda and subdivide into groups of four for the Bible Study time. Count off around the group: "one, two, one, two"—and have the "ones" move quickly to another room for sharing.

**What is the long-term expectation of the group for mission?**

To grow the size of the group and eventually start a new group after one or two years.

**What do you do when the group does not want to multiply?**

This is the reason why this MISSION needs to be discussed at the beginning of a group—not at the end. If the group is committed to this MISSION at the outset, and works on this mission in stage one, they will be ready for multiplication at the end of the final stage.

**What are the principles behind the Serendipity approach to Bible Study for a beginner group?**

1. *Level the Playing Field.* Start the sharing with things that are easy to talk about and where everyone is equal—things that are instantly recallable—light, mischievously revealing and childlike. Meet at the human side before moving into spiritual things.

2. *Share Your Spiritual Story.* Group Building, especially for new groups, is essential. It is crucial for Bible Study in beginner groups to help the group become a community by giving everyone the opportunity to share their spiritual history.

3. *Open Questions / Right Brain.* Open-ended questions are better than closed questions. Open questions allow for options, observations and a variety of opinions in which no one is right or wrong. Similarly, "right-brained" questions are

better than "left-brained" questions. Right-brained questions seek out your first impressions, tone, motives and subjective feelings about the text. Right-brained questions work well with narratives. Multiple-choice questionnaires encourage people who know very little about the Bible. Given a set of multiple-choice options, a new believer is not threatened, and a shy person is not intimidated. Everyone has something to contribute.

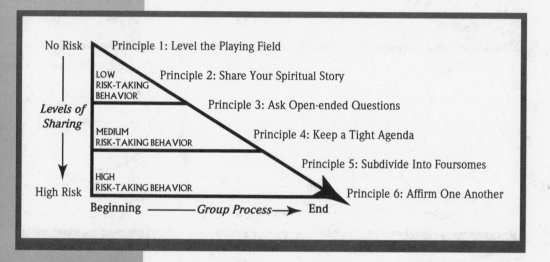

No Risk — Principle 1: Level the Playing Field

LOW RISK-TAKING BEHAVIOR — Principle 2: Share Your Spiritual Story

Principle 3: Ask Open-ended Questions

*Levels of Sharing*

MEDIUM RISK-TAKING BEHAVIOR — Principle 4: Keep a Tight Agenda

Principle 5: Subdivide Into Foursomes

HIGH RISK-TAKING BEHAVIOR

High Risk — Principle 6: Affirm One Another

Beginning ——— *Group Process* → End

**4. Tight Agenda.** A tight agenda is better than a loose agenda for beginning small groups. Those people who might be nervous about "sharing" will find comfort knowing that the meeting agenda has been carefully organized. The more structure the first few meetings have the better, especially for a new group. Some people are afraid that a structured agenda will limit discussion. In fact, the opposite is true. The Serendipity agenda is designed to keep the discussion focused on what's important and to bring out genuine feelings, issues, and areas of need. If the goal is to move the group toward deeper relationships and a deeper experience of God, then a structured agenda is the best way to achieve that goal.

**5. Fearless Foursomes.** Dividing your small group into foursomes during the Bible Study can be a good idea. In groups of four, everyone will have an opportunity to participate and you can finish the Bible Study in 30 minutes. In groups of eight or more, the Bible Study will need to be longer and you will take away from the Caring Time.

Also, by subdividing into groups of four for the Bible Study time, you give others a chance to develop their skills at leading a group—in preparation for the day when you develop a small cell to eventually move out and birth a new group.

6. *Affirm the person and their story.* Give positive feedback to group members: "Thank you for sharing ... " "Your story really helps me to understand where you are coming from ... " "Your story was a real gift to me ... " This affirmation given honestly will create the atmosphere for deeper sharing.

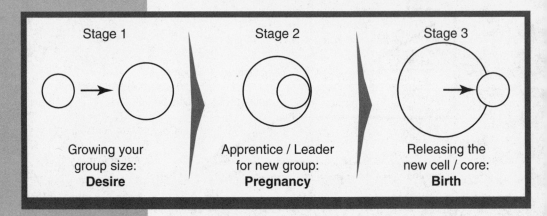

| Stage 1 | Stage 2 | Stage 3 |
|---------|---------|---------|
| Growing your group size: **Desire** | Apprentice / Leader for new group: **Pregnancy** | Releasing the new cell / core: **Birth** |

**What is the next stage of our group all about?**

In the next stage, the 201 BIBLE STUDY is deeper, GROUP BUILDING focuses on developing your gifts, and in the MISSION you will identify an Apprentice / Leader and two others within your group who will eventually become the leadership core of a new group down the road a bit.

# Caring Time / 15–45 Minutes

LEADER:
Ask the
group, "Who
are you going
to invite for
next week?"

During your time of prayer, remember the people who shared and what they said. If you don't know how to begin, finish this sentence:

*"Dear God, I want to talk with you about my friend ..."*

Don't forget to keep praying for the empty chair and inviting people to your group.

## Reference Notes

**Summary.** Paul continues his discussion of the three basic sets of relationships which dominate most people's lives (he had just addressed the relationship between wives and husbands). Here he deals with relationships within a family (between parents and children), and the relationship between slaves and masters. Paul begins by urging children to "obey," and then gives four reasons for such obedience: (1) they are "in the Lord"; (2) it is the "right" thing to do; (3) God commands obedience; and (4) obedience brings a rich reward. Parents are then urged to limit the exercise of their authority and to train their children in the ways of the Lord. To slaves Paul says, in essence, "Come to view your work as service to Christ, and thus labor for your master in the same way that you would labor for the Lord." To masters Paul says, in essence, "The slave is a person who is to be treated as you expect to be treated, since before God you are both equal."

**6:1–3** Paul does not simply command obedience on the part of children. He gives reasons for it. In other words, Paul does not take obedience for granted. In the same way that he addressed husbands and wives (and gave each a rationale for their behavior), he does the same for children.

**6:1 *Children.*** The very fact that Paul even addresses children is amazing. Normally, all such instructions would come via their parents. That he addresses children in this public letter means that children were in attendance with their families at worship when such a letter would have been read. Paul does not define a "child" here; i.e., he does not deal with the question of when a child becomes an adult and thus ceases to be under parental authority. This is not a real problem, however, since each culture has its own definition of when adulthood begins. Even as adults, however, children are expected to "honor" their parents.

***obey.*** Paul tells children to "obey" ("follow," "be subject to," literally, "listen to"). He uses a different word from the one used when speaking of

33

the relationship between wives and husbands. Parents have authority over their children, but not husbands over wives. Also, although "obey" is a stronger word than "submit," it is not without limits.

***in the Lord.*** This is the first reason children are to obey their parents. There are two ways in which this phrase can be taken: Obey your parents because you are a Christian, and/or obey your parents in everything that is compatible with your commitment to Christ.

***for this is right.*** This is the second of four reasons Paul gives for obedience. "Children obey parents. That is simply the way it is," Paul says. It is not confined to Christian ethics; it is standard behavior in any society. Pagan moralists, both Greek and Roman, taught it. Stoic philosophers saw a son's obedience as self-prudent, plainly required by reason and part of the "nature of things."

**6:2** ***"Honor your father and mother."*** Paul begins to quote the fifth commandment. This is the third reason children should obey parents. God commands it. "To honor father and mother means more than to obey them, especially if this obedience is interpreted in a merely outward sense. It is the inner attitude of the child toward his parents that comes to the fore in the requirement that he honor them. All selfish obedience or reluctant obedience or obedience under terror is immediately ruled out. To honor implies to love, to regard highly, to show the spirit of respect and consideration. This honor is to be shown to both of the parents, for as far as the child is concerned they are equal in authority" (Hendriksen).

***the first commandment with a promise.*** Paul probably means "first in importance," since the second commandment (Ex. 20:4–6) promises God's love to those who love God. It has been argued by F. F. Bruce, however, that the second commandment does not contain a promise but a statement of God's character.

**6:3** This is the fourth reason for obedience. It produces good rewards. Here Paul identifies the two aspects of the promise. It involved material well-being and long life. The promise is probably not for individual children, but for the community of which they are a part. It will be prosperous and long-standing.

**6:4** Just as children have a duty to obey, parents have the duty to instruct children with gentleness and restraint.

***Fathers.*** The model for a father is that of God the "Father of all" (Eph. 4:6). In the way that he drew together people from diverse tribes and nations into one loving community (Eph. 3:14–15), so too human fathers are to exercise this kind of love. This view of fatherhood stands in sharp contrast to the harsh Roman father, who had the power of life and death over his children.

***exasperate.*** Parents are to be responsible for not provoking hostility on the part of their children. By humiliating children, being cruel to them, overindulging them, or being unreasonable, parents squash children (rather than encourage them).

***bring them up.*** This verb is literally "nourish" or "feed" them.

***training.*** This word can be translated "discipline," and "is training with the accent on the correction of the young" (Houlden).

***instruction.*** The emphasis here is on what is said verbally to children.

**6:5–8** That Paul should even address slaves is amazing. In the first century, they were often considered more akin to farm animals than human beings, the only difference being that they could talk. Slaves were "living tools" according to Aristotle. Yet Paul speaks to them as people able to choose and to decide—quite revolutionary for his era. Paul addresses these slaves in the context of the worship service where his letter would have been read. Women, children and slaves were all, apparently, participants in Christian worship. This is an example of what Paul was speaking about in the first half of his letter when he points to the new body—the church—into which Christ was gathering all peoples, regardless of who they were.

**6:5 *obey.*** Paul is not counseling rebellion (an impossibility in any case—given the conditions of the first century—and a cause which could lead only to massive bloodshed). The word "obey" is the same one which Paul used to define the child's duty to the parent.

***earthly.*** As opposed to "heavenly." Paul reminds slaves that although they may be "owned" by another human being at the moment, ultimately they belong to Christ, who is their true Lord.

***with sincerity of heart.*** Or "with singleness of heart." Slaves are to give their masters the same wholehearted devotion they would give to the Lord.

**6:6 *not only to win their favor when their eye is on you.*** This is a good rendering of the phrase which reads literally, "not by way of eye-service as men-pleasers." In other words, don't just pretend to be serving wholeheartedly when, in fact, you only work when you are watched (and then simply to gain favor with your master).

**6:9 *Do not threaten them.*** In the same way that parents are not to exasperate children, masters are not to browbeat slaves. Punishment was the usual way of controlling slaves. Paul says, "Don't even use threats against the powerless."

SESSION

# 5

# Parents in Pain

**3-PART AGENDA**

**ICE-BREAKER**
15 Minutes

**BIBLE STUDY**
30 Minutes

**CARING TIME**
15–45 Minutes

Even the most loving families experience friction when people live under the same roof. Some of this conflict is usually just light banter and produces little hostility or pain. The strains of keeping a marriage healthy, raising children and making ends meet combine to make fertile soil for family conflict. Who's going to feed the baby at 3 a.m.? Who tracked mud all over the newly scrubbed kitchen floor? Who's been squeezing the toothpaste tube in the middle? Who splurged on new spring clothes and wiped out the family budget?

But some of the conflict cuts to the heart of who we are. Children feel misunderstood or not taken seriously. Parents feel as if they aren't being respected, or they feel uncertain as to what to do next. If such conflict is not dealt with in a redemptive manner, family conflict can cause deep pain well into the children's adulthood.

> **LEADER: If you haven't already, now is the time to start thinking about the next step for your group. Take a look at the 201 courses (the second stage in the small group life cycle) on the inside of the back cover.**

Family conflict does not have to blow a family apart. Through loving patience and understanding, conflict can actually draw a family together. Communication is the key. Solutions to conflict can usually be found when members are able to freely talk and listen without being devastated. Sometimes, however, outside help is needed, and a family certainly should not be ashamed to call on a minister or professional counselor when necessary.

In the Option 1 Study (from Luke's Gospel), we will see a father's pain and a son's rebellion turn into a tearful reunion. And in the Option 2 Study (from Paul's second letter to the Corinthians), we will see how Paul dealt with his "parental pain" regarding this church. The particular purpose of the Bible Study is to talk about the pain in your life as a parent.

# Ice-Breaker / 15 Minutes

**Lessons in Conflict.** Take a few minutes and share your responses to the following questions.

*1.* Looking back, what was the funniest thing you did as a teenager that got you in trouble with your parents?

*2.* What important thing did you learn in conflicts with your parents?
- ❏ Always apologize (even if you're right!).
- ❏ Father (and mother) knows best.
- ❏ It's best to talk it out.
- ❏ Even parents can be wrong sometimes.
- ❏ What your parents don't know won't hurt them (or you either!).
- ❏ Listening to each other clears up many conflicts.
- ❏ It's better to face a conflict and get it over with than to try to hide or ignore it.
- ❏ other:_____

*3.* In your normal style of handling conflict, which are you more like?
- ❏ an ostrich—I hide my head in the sand until the conflict goes away.
- ❏ a house dog—I timidly slouch away, then chew up the couch when no one's looking.
- ❏ a hawk—I fly above it all and pick my targets.
- ❏ a fox—I use my brains to win.
- ❏ a dolphin—I can fight if necessary, but would rather swim away.

# Bible Study / 30 Minutes

## Option 1 / Gospel Study

## Luke 15:11–32 / Fracas in the Family

The story of the Prodigal Son is one of the best-known passages in the Bible. Not surprisingly, this parable provides useful insights into the way one relates to our older children, especially when they act in ways that are destructive or short-sighted. Before we examine this passage, however, a note of caution is in order. Jesus' purpose in telling this story was not to guide parents in the way to deal with wayward kids. This parable is open to various interpretations, depending on where the chief focus is thought to be. For instance, as the Parable of the Lost Son, it shows the process of repentance and the joy that awaits the sinner who will turn to God. As the Parable of the Older Son, it forces the Pharisees to consider the meaning of their own hostility to Jesus' reception of the tax collectors and sinners (Luke 15:1–2). As the Parable of the Loving Father, it illustrates the boundless, lavish love of God toward his wayward children. We will approach the story from this latter vantage point, focusing on the father (and his actions and attitudes), and using the story as a case study that helps us to reflect on ways of responding to our children. Read Luke 15:11–32 and discuss your responses to the following questions with your group.

*11Jesus continued: "There was a man who had two sons. 12The younger one said to his father, 'Father, give me my share of the estate.' So he divided his property between them.*

*13"Not long after that, the younger son got together all he had, set off for a distant country and there squandered his wealth in wild living. 14After he had spent everything, there was a severe famine in that whole country, and he began to be in need. 15So he went and hired himself out to a citizen of that country, who sent him to his fields to feed pigs. 16He longed to fill his stomach with the pods that the pigs were eating, but no one gave him anything.*

*17"When he came to his senses, he said, 'How many of my father's hired men have food to spare, and here I am starving to death! 18I will set out and go back to my father and say to him: Father, I have sinned against heaven and against you. 19I am no longer worthy to be called your son; make me like one of your hired men.' 20So he got up and went to his father.*

*"But while he was still a long way off, his father saw him and was filled with compassion for him; he ran to his son, threw his arms around him and kissed him.*

*21"The son said to him, 'Father, I have sinned against heaven and against you. I am no longer worthy to be called your son.'*

*22"But the father said to his servants, 'Quick! Bring the best robe and put it on him. Put a ring on his finger and sandals on his feet. 23Bring the fattened calf and kill it. Let's have a feast and celebrate. 24For this son of mine was dead and is alive again; he was lost and is found.' So they began to celebrate.*

*25"Meanwhile, the older son was in the field. When he came near the house, he heard music and dancing. 26So he called one of the servants and asked him what was going on. 27'Your brother has come,' he replied, 'and your father has killed the fattened calf because he has him back safe and sound.'*

*28"The older brother became angry and refused to go in. So his father went out and pleaded with him. 29But he answered his father, 'Look! All these years I've been slaving for you and never disobeyed your orders. Yet you never gave me even a young goat so I could celebrate with my friends.*

*30But when this son of yours who has squandered your property with prostitutes comes home, you kill the fattened calf for him!'*

*31" 'My son,' the father said, 'you are always with me, and everything I have is yours. 32But we had to celebrate and be glad, because this brother of yours was dead and is alive again; he was lost and is found.' "*

1. Which relationship in your family generates the most conflict—and what is the general nature of that conflict?
   - ❒ father and son
   - ❒ mother and son
   - ❒ father and daughter
   - ❒ mother and daughter
   - ❒ brother and brother
   - ❒ sister and brother
   - ❒ sister and sister
   - ❒ husband and wife

2. If you had been the father in this Bible story, what would you have said to the younger son when he asked for his inheritance early in order to leave home?
   - ❒ "Are you crazy?!"
   - ❒ "Why you ungrateful ...!!"
   - ❒ "Well, I'm disappointed, but here you are."
   - ❒ "No problem, son."

3. If you had been the father and had a pretty good idea where your son had gone, would you have gone after him?
   - ❒ Yes, you don't want to see your kid get in trouble.
   - ❒ Maybe, if I thought I could get him to come home.
   - ❒ No, you have to let people make their own mistakes.
   - ❒ It all depends.

4. When the younger son returned home, what would have been your attitude?
   - ❒ "Good to see you—but you're grounded!"
   - ❒ "You have disgraced the family."
   - ❒ "Where's the money?"
   - ❒ "I don't approve of your actions, but you're still my son."
   - ❒ "Welcome home, son—I love you!"

5. How would you have reacted when the older son protested?
   - ❒ agreed with him and canceled the party
   - ❒ told him to lighten up
   - ❒ advised him to spend a little time in a foreign country himself
   - ❒ appealed to his love for his brother
   - ❒ promised him a party of his own

6. What does this story teach us about how God relates to us as our heavenly Father? What does this imply for our role as parents?

"The
problems of
America are
the family
problems
multiplied a
million-fold."
—Dwight D.
Eisenhower

7. How does your relationship to God the Father affect the pain you experience as a parent?
   ❐ It helps me know that God experiences the same pain in relation to us.
   ❐ It helps me know that God will give me the strength I need.
   ❐ It helps me know that my children are ultimately in God's hands.
   ❐ It does not affect my pain one way or another.

8. Which of the father's qualities do you most need?
   ❐ his willingness to let his son make mistakes
   ❐ his patience in waiting for change
   ❐ his capacity to forgive
   ❐ his understanding in dealing with both his children
   ❐ his ability to celebrate life

## Option 2 / Epistle Study

## 2 Corinthians 1:23–2:4 / Painful Times

Paul had a painful and troubled relationship with the church at Corinth, and this relationship seems to have generated more letters than Paul wrote to any other church. Central sources of those conflicts were their divisions as a church and their questioning of his authority. This passage (from one of his letters) expresses his feelings about those conflicts. Read 2 Corinthians 1:23–2:4 and discuss your responses to the following questions with your group.

*²³I call God as my witness that it was in order to spare you that I did not return to Corinth. ²⁴Not that we lord it over your faith, but we work with you* **2** *for your joy, because it is by faith you stand firm. ¹So I made up my mind that I would not make another painful visit to you. ²For if I grieve you, who is left to make me glad but you whom I have grieved? ³I wrote as I did so that when I came I should not be distressed by those who ought to make me rejoice. I had confidence in all of you, that you would all share my joy. ⁴For I wrote you out of great distress and anguish of heart and with many tears, not to grieve you but to let you know the depth of my love for you.*

1. Which word would you use to describe Paul's feelings as he wrote this passage?
   ❐ angry                    ❐ defensive
   ❐ hurt                      ❐ loving
   ❐ sad                       ❐ grief-stricken

2. What causes most parents the greatest pain?
   - ❏ their overwhelming responsibilities
   - ❏ their inability to make decisions
   - ❏ their lack of self-confidence
   - ❏ disrespectful children
   - ❏ irresponsible children
   - ❏ disobedient children
   - ❏ other:_____

3. How did your parents exercise authority over you in your childhood years?
   - ❏ I knew who was in charge of any situation—they were.
   - ❏ They loved and disciplined me in fair ways.
   - ❏ Their love and discipline provided me with a lot of freedom.
   - ❏ They controlled every situation (and me).
   - ❏ There was more discipline than love.
   - ❏ I always knew that they were my parents, but they allowed me to make my own decisions.
   - ❏ other:_____

4. How do you (plan to) exercise authority over your children?
   - ❏ let them know that I am in charge
   - ❏ love and discipline them in fair ways
   - ❏ love and discipline them with a lot of freedom
   - ❏ control them (and every situation)
   - ❏ with strict discipline, less love
   - ❏ let them know that I am their parent, but allow them to make their own decisions
   - ❏ other:_____

5. How should discipline change when a child enters the teenage years?
   - ❏ Less physical discipline should be used, and more restriction and social discipline.
   - ❏ More freedom to choose should be allowed.
   - ❏ Parents should talk more about the reasons behind rules and discipline.
   - ❏ Parents need to help children learn self-discipline.
   - ❏ Parents have to be even tougher.
   - ❏ Discipline should not change when children reach this age.
   - ❏ other:_____

6. When have you experienced what Paul discussed here (vv. 2–4)—when what was meant as an expression of love for his "children" caused them grief? What did you do to clarify your intent and find healing in the relationship?

**7.** How prepared were (or are) you for the troublesome times with your children?

**8.** What can you do to be more prepared for those troubling times?

**COMMENT** The background of this passage is important. Paul had a rather tumultuous relationship with the Corinthian church. During his first visit to Corinth, he founded the church. However, after he left the city, he heard that the new Christians there were engaged in a variety of activities that were clearly outside the bounds of the Gospel. They had split into warring factions, they were really confused about sexuality, they were taking each other to court, and so on. So he wrote a letter to them (1 Corinthians), challenging them about what was going on in the church. In that letter, Paul promised to return to visit them again (1 Cor. 16:1–9). His return visit, however, proved extremely painful (because of the conflict he had with a false apostle who had begun teaching in Corinth). What really disturbed Paul was that the Corinthian Christians did not rally to support him in this conflict.

It is unclear exactly what took place next, but it seems that Paul sent various letters in order to correct the situation. We read in 2 Corinthians that Paul was anxiously awaiting news as to whether the problem in Corinth had finally been resolved. He was so concerned about the situation that he left Troas and took a boat across to Macedonia to be nearer to Corinth (and thus to receive news that much sooner).

# Caring Time / 15–45 Minutes

Take time at the close to share any personal prayer requests. Answer the question:

**LEADER:**
**Ask the group, "Who are you going to invite for next week?"**

*"How can we help you in prayer this week?"*

Then go around and let each person pray for the person on their right. Finish the sentence,

> *"Dear God, I want to speak to you about my friend _____."*

As you close, include a prayer for the bonding of your group members, as well as for the numerical growth of the group.

**1:23** Having alluded to their common commitment to Christ (2 Cor. 1:18–22), Paul returns to his main thought (2 Cor. 1:17).

*God as my witness.* This is a solemn declaration by which Paul calls upon God as a witness to what he says.

*to spare you.* While some implied that Paul's change in plans was a result of ulterior motives, Paul asserts he was thinking of the Corinthians, not himself, when he changed his plans.

**1:24** Lest verse 23 make it sound as though Paul viewed himself as a spiritual dictator planning to exercise control over the Corinthians, he points out that he is dedicated to working for their joy.

**2:1** *another painful visit.* During this earlier visit, Paul was resisted or slandered by a member of the church itself (2 Cor. 2:5–11). This was probably not one of the itinerant teachers (who may not have yet arrived). While the offense was committed by one individual, the church's sin was that it failed to take any action, which implied their lack of respect for Paul as a minister of the Gospel. This hurt Paul, creating a rift between him and the church.

**2:2–3** *glad / rejoice.* Paul writes as if the relationship between he and the Corinthians is fundamentally sound, despite the temporary pain during his second visit.

**2:3** *I wrote.* Paul was in a bind. If he came again as proposed, he would cause pain. If he didn't come, he would be charged with "fickleness." The middle course was to write, hoping perhaps thereby to rectify the problem. So he wrote his third (now lost) letter, the so-called "sorrowful" letter.

*I should not be distressed.* Paul is concerned both that they will be grieved by another visit (vv. 1–2), and that he too will find it painful. His fear, perhaps, is that indeed they had been subverted by the false apostles and had embraced a false gospel.

**2:4** Paul's intention for his third letter was not to cause the Corinthians to be distressed, but simply to share his great pain (as a result of the situation) and his great love for them.

# Parental Expectations

Excessive stress is epidemic in our society, and families are not immune to it. Frazzled parents escape the wear-and-tear of the workplace only to come home to the stressful demands of the family. The innocence of childhood is often interrupted by the gut-wrenching sound of parents fighting. And the balance in the checkbook never seems to move very far from zero. But while every family experiences some stress, the home can often be a sanctuary from stress. Studies have shown that many men and women believe their family life counterbalances job stress.

Sometimes stress is caused by unrealistic expectations. Everyone dreams about their ideal life. And occasionally, we all play the "if only ..." game. Parents are no different. Often, in wanting the best for their children, the parents' expectations may get in the way of what the child really wants. This is often demonstrated at athletic events for kids, when their over-zealous parents become the expert coach or referee.

**LEADER: This is the next to last session in this course. At the end of the course, how would you like to celebrate your time together? With a dinner? With a party? With a commitment to continue as a group?**

It's natural for parents to want the best for their kids. And it's natural for parents to expect certain things from their children. But stress and tension mount when parental expectations take over and differ with their children's wishes (and maybe even God's plans).

In the Option 1 Study, this is precisely what happened with the mother of James and John. We will study how Jesus handled this situation in Matthew's Gospel. In the Option 2 Study (from Paul's letter to the Colossians), we will discover God's expectations for us. Remember, in these sessions, the issue is your life as a parent. Use the Scripture passages to walk into your story with your group.

To get started, take a few minutes and share about expectations in your family by doing the following ice-breaker.

# Ice-Breaker / 15 Minutes

**Family Expectations.** Complete the following sentences and share them with your group. If you don't have time to do all three questions, skip the second one.

*1.* I FEEL LIKE MY PARENTS EXPECTED ME TO BE ...
- ❏ the next president
- ❏ an incredible success
- ❏ completely obedient
- ❏ the next Albert Einstein
- ❏ a golden boy/girl
- ❏ a straight "A" student
- ❏ a compensation for their failures
- ❏ a great athlete
- ❏ a great musician
- ❏ just like them
- ❏ perfect
- ❏ self-sufficient
- ❏ whatever made me happy
- ❏ other:_____

*2.* I FEEL LIKE MY PARENTS LOOK (OR LOOKED) UPON ME AS ...
- ❏ a troublesome kid
- ❏ a scapegoat
- ❏ a security blanket
- ❏ their pride and joy
- ❏ a disappointment
- ❏ a wonderful person
- ❏ a continuation of themselves
- ❏ a helpless baby
- ❏ glue
- ❏ a capable adult
- ❏ a liability
- ❏ invisible
- ❏ good stock
- ❏ other:_____

*3.* I FEEL LIKE MY CHILDREN SEE ME AS ...
- ❏ a role model
- ❏ their enemy
- ❏ a pushover
- ❏ the great provider
- ❏ a household slave
- ❏ a source of love
- ❏ a complete fool
- ❏ a friend
- ❏ a bag of money
- ❏ godlike
- ❏ a chauffeur
- ❏ other:_____

# Bible Study / 30 Minutes

## Option 1 / Gospel Study

## Matthew 20:20–28 / A Mother's Request

This incident occurred late in Jesus' earthly ministry, and details the disciples "jockeying for position" at a time when they expected Jesus' kingdom to come soon. Read Matthew 20:20–28, and discuss your responses to the following questions with your group.

²⁰*Then the mother of Zebedee's sons came to Jesus with her sons and, kneeling down, asked a favor of him.*

²¹*"What is it you want?" he asked.*

*She said, "Grant that one of these two sons of mine may sit at your right and the other at your left in your kingdom."*

²²*"You don't know what you are asking," Jesus said to them. "Can you drink the cup I am going to drink?"*

*"We can," they answered.*

²³*Jesus said to them, "You will indeed drink from my cup, but to sit at my right or left is not for me to grant. These places belong to those for whom they have been prepared by my Father."*

²⁴*When the ten heard about this, they were indignant with the two brothers. ²⁵Jesus called them together and said, "You know that the rulers of the Gentiles lord it over them, and their high officials exercise authority over them. ²⁶Not so with you. Instead, whoever wants to become great among you must be your servant, ²⁷and whoever wants to be first must be your slave— ²⁸just as the Son of Man did not come to be served, but to serve, and to give his life as a ransom for many."*

*1.* Who is the most competitive person in your family? Do you see competitiveness as a positive or negative quality?

*2.* Who are you most embarrassed for in this story?
❐ Jesus—for having to refuse the mother's request
❐ the mother of the two sons
❐ the two sons—James and John

*3.* Why do you think the mother did this?
❐ Her two sons put her up to it.
❐ She was just acting like a mother.
❐ She wanted the best for her sons.
❐ She was focused on her own sense of pride and satisfaction.
❐ She didn't realize what she was asking.

*4.* These brothers turned out to be significant leaders in the church. How much credit do you give their mother for this?
❐ a whole lot
❐ a little
❐ quite a bit
❐ none

**5.** What is the closest your mother (or father) came to embarrassing you in public?
❏ insisting that I "perform" for the relatives
❏ showing my baby pictures to my girlfriend or boyfriend
❏ coming to a school event and clapping or cheering too loudly
❏ telling a secret family story to my high school friends
❏ crying at my wedding
❏ other: _____

**6.** Which of the following comes closest to the truth concerning your parents' expectations of you?
❏ My parents expected very little, causing me to doubt my ability.
❏ My parents expected perfection, causing me to be dissatisfied with all I did.
❏ My parents' expectations were high enough to challenge me, and low enough to be reachable.
❏ My parents helped me to develop my own set of expectations.

**7.** Are you living up to your parents' expectations?
❏ Are you kidding?!          ❏ I quit trying.
❏ I'm trying.                ❏ Yes.
❏ I think I am exceeding their expectations for me.
❏ My parents didn't lay any expectations on me.

**8.** Regarding expectations, what issues cause the most stress or conflict in your family? (Choose the top three.)

| | |
|---|---|
| ___ household duties | ___ friends |
| ___ schedules / use of time | ___ money / spending |
| ___ use of television / telephone | ___ discipline |
| ___ personal appearance | ___ future plans |
| ___ church involvement | ___ curfew |
| ___ drugs, alcohol, tobacco | ___ manners |
| ___ entertainment choices | ___ language |
| ___ schoolwork / grades | ___ respect |

**9.** As you read what Jesus told this mother, what does it imply for you about your expectations for your children?
❏ I need to stop being a "stage mother."
❏ I need to stop speaking on behalf of my children and let them speak on their own behalf.
❏ I need to help my children focus less on self-glory and more on how they can serve.
❏ Before I encourage my children to reach for something, I should be sure I know the cost.
❏ other:_____

**10.** What would you like to pass on to your kids?

❒ nothing in particular—They need to develop on their own.

❒ a sense of right and wrong

❒ a deep faith

❒ lots of initiative

❒ loyalty to the family

❒ unconditional acceptance

❒ significant wealth

❒ other:_____

**11.** How will you pass these things on to your kids?

## Option 2 / Epistle Study

## Colossians 3:1–17 / God's Expectations

This letter was written to the church at Colosse, which was a Greek city. At that time, Greeks did not have high moral expectations of people, especially with respect to sexual morality. In this passage, Paul sets some higher expectations for them. Read Colossians 3:1–17 and discuss your responses to the following questions with your group.

**3** *Since, then, you have been raised with Christ, set your hearts on things above, where Christ is seated at the right hand of God. ²Set your minds on things above, not on earthly things. ³For you died, and your life is now hidden with Christ in God. ⁴When Christ, who is your life, appears, then you also will appear with him in glory.*

*⁵Put to death, therefore, whatever belongs to your earthly nature: sexual immorality, impurity, lust, evil desires and greed, which is idolatry. ⁶Because of these, the wrath of God is coming. ⁷You used to walk in these ways, in the life you once lived. ⁸But now you must rid yourselves of all such things as these: anger, rage, malice, slander, and filthy language from your lips. ⁹Do not lie to each other, since you have taken off your old self with its practices ¹⁰and have put on the new self, which is being renewed in knowledge in the image of its Creator. ¹¹Here there is no Greek or Jew, circumcised or uncircumcised, barbarian, Scythian, slave or free, but Christ is all, and is in all.*

*¹²Therefore, as God's chosen people, holy and dearly loved, clothe yourselves with compassion, kindness, humility, gentleness and patience. ¹³Bear with each other and forgive whatever grievances you may have against one another. Forgive as the Lord forgave you. ¹⁴And over all these virtues put on love, which binds them all together in perfect unity.*

*[15]Let the peace of Christ rule in your hearts, since as members of one body you were called to peace. And be thankful. [16]Let the word of Christ dwell in you richly as you teach and admonish one another with all wisdom, and as you sing psalms, hymns and spiritual songs with gratitude in your hearts to God. [17]And whatever you do, whether in word or deed, do it all in the name of the Lord Jesus, giving thanks to God the Father through him.*

1. If you were hearing Paul's letter for the first time, would you feel more encouraged—or discouraged—by these high standards and expectations?

2. How much contrast is there between the "earthly nature" (vv. 5–11) and God's expectations for his people (vv. 12–17)?

3. How does one go about making the switch?

4. Growing up, how did your parents' expectations differ from your expectations for yourself?
   ❐ Their expectations were much higher (or harder) than mine.
   ❐ Their expectations were much lower (or easier) than mine.
   ❐ We shared similar expectations.
   ❐ My parents never had expectations for me.
   ❐ It didn't matter to me what they expected.

> "God does not expect us to imitate Jesus Christ. He expects us to allow the life of Jesus to be manifested."
> —Oswald Chambers

5. Using one word or a short phrase, what are your expectations of your children in each of these areas:

   morally _____

   relationally _____

   spiritually _____

   educationally _____

   in achievements _____

   in behavior toward me _____

6. How do your expectations for your children mesh with God's expectations, as seen in this Scripture passage?
   ❐ They are one and the same.
   ❐ There is significant overlap.
   ❐ There are some similarities.
   ❐ They are vastly different.

7. What can you do to help your children accept or meet God's expectations for them?

Most parents have expectations for their children, whether or not the parents express them. One of the questions parents need to ask themselves is whether their expectations coincide or conflict with God's expectations.

As Christians, we are to pattern our lives on God's ways—not the ways of the world. Every day we need to move away from attitudes and actions which reflect our old way of life. In verses 5–9 of this passage, Paul lists sins that God expects us to give up in our lives. Although this isn't an easy command to follow, God's Spirit is ready and able to help us make tough choices.

But that is not all. Paul continues (in vv. 12–17) to outline God's expectations for us about the way we ought to live. Again, the Spirit who is in us can help us to fulfill these expectations. Periodically, we need to check and see if our expectations are in line with God's expectations. If they aren't, stress and strain are bound to exist—complicating our lives even further.

# Caring Time / 15–45 Minutes

Take time at the close to share any personal prayer requests. Answer the question:

*"How can we help you in prayer this week?"*

Then go around and let each person pray for the person on their right. Finish the sentence:

*"Dear God, I want to speak to you about
my friend _____."*

P.S.
If the next session is your last session together, you may want to plan a party to celebrate your time together. Save a few minutes at the close of this session to make these plans.

**3:1 raised with Christ.** As the Christian's death "with Christ" cut the bonds to the old authorities (Col. 2:20), so one's life "with Christ" creates new bonds with God and others.

**set your hearts.** Literally, "seek."

**on things above.** This is not encouraging escapism from earthly affairs. The point is that Christians are to shape their lives by the values of the heavenly world in which Christ sits enthroned as King, rather than heeding rules based on the elemental spirits.

**3:2 Set your minds.** "... orient your life by" (Reumann).

**3:3 hidden with Christ.** Christian spirituality is not outwardly flashy (like that of the false teachers in Colosse). Its fullness comes when Christ appears (v. 4), not now. But, while the Christian's life is full of ups and downs, one who submits their life to Christ is in no danger of losing it.

**3:5–14** The instructions in these verses are based on a common set of ethical teachings, used to instruct converts in the way of Christ. The "put off" and "put on" metaphors may relate to the putting off and putting on of new clothes at a convert's baptism.

**3:5 Put to death.** Believers are to work out their death and resurrection with Christ (Col. 2:12,20; 3:1) by daily turning away from attitudes and actions that reflect the old way of life.

**3:8 rid yourselves of all such things.** Immorality, greed, abusive talk, etc. have no place in the life of a Christian. To repent means to consciously work at removing them from one's life.

**3:9 taken off your old self.** Literally, "to strip off." This phrase is used to describe the putting off of the sinful nature through Christ's death (Col. 2:11) and Christ's victory over the powers (Col. 2:15).

**3:10 put on the new self.** The lifestyle of Christians is patterned after the attitudes and actions of Christ who is at work within them (1 Cor. 15:45; Gal. 3:27).

**3:11 Scythian.** The Greeks considered Scythians to be especially uncouth barbarians. Allegiance to Christ eradicates prideful divisions based on race, religion, culture or social class (and gender—Gal. 3:28).

**3:12–17** Paul uses the image of putting on new clothes to show how true spirituality involves "wearing" the Christlike qualities of love, peace and thankfulness (see Rom.13:14).

**3:14 *over all these virtues put on love.*** According to Jesus, to love God and others is the sum total of the meaning of the Law (Mark 12:30–31).

**3:15 *Let the peace of Christ rule in your hearts.*** "Your" is plural: What is in view is not a sense of personal serenity, but a mutual commitment to consider peaceful relationships with one another as the highest priority in their corporate life.

***called to peace.*** While the reconciliation of people with God and one another is the major theme of Christian doctrine (Col. 1:20–22; 2:2; 3:9–11), living out this reconciliation is the major emphasis of Christian ethics (Rom. 14:19–15:7; Gal. 5:22–26; Col. 3:12–14).

***be thankful.*** Thankfulness for God's grace is the central motive of Christian living (Col. 1:12; 3:16–17; 4:2).

**3:16 *the word of Christ.*** While the false teachers have "lost connection with the Head" (Col. 2:19), the message the Colossians teach one another must be centered on Jesus.

***dwell in you richly.*** This is a form of the word for "fullness." Spiritual fullness is rooted neither in secret knowledge nor in mystical experiences, but in a commitment to Christ.

***teach / sing.*** Literally, "teaching and admonishing one another in psalms, hymns and spiritual songs." Rather than referring to two distinct activities (teaching and singing), Paul is referring to worship services where the people shared their knowledge of God through singing to one another.

***psalms, hymns and spiritual songs.*** The psalms are the Old Testament Psalms. Hymns were songs common to the church (examples may be Luke 1:46–55; 1:68–79; John 1:1–18; Eph. 5:14; Phil. 2:6–11; Rev. 4:11). Spiritual songs were spontaneous expressions of praise to Christ.

**3:17** This summary sentence shows that the ethical core of Christianity is not a set of rules, but a commitment to reflect the values and character of Jesus in whatever situation one encounters. Christ, who rules over all creation (v. 1), is also the model people are to imitate in all areas of life.

# Family of God

**3-PART AGENDA**

**ICE-BREAKER**
15 Minutes

**BIBLE STUDY**
30 Minutes

**CARING TIME**
15–45 Minutes

The Bible uses the analogy of the family to describe the relationship of Christians to God, and of Christians to each other. Jesus taught that if we do God's will, we are his "brothers and sisters." Christians are often described in Scripture as the "children of God" and the "sons [daughters] of God." In their New Testament writings, the apostles Paul, James and John each address their fellow Christians as brothers and sisters.

The representation of the Christian church as the family of God is intentional. The family has been an enduring part of virtually every civilization. The family is the showcase for parental love. The family is the cocoon within which children grow and mature. The family provides an environment where love can germinate and flourish.

In the Option 1 Study (from Mark's Gospel), Jesus defines the members of the family of God. And in the Option 2 Study (from the letter to the Ephesians), Paul describes how God has created his family out of diverse people, from those who were once enemies. In both passages, the important point is that we become members of God's family through Jesus Christ—specifically (as Paul shows) as a result of Christ's death on the cross.

**LEADER: Read the bottom part of page M8 in the center section concerning future mission possibilities for your group. Save plenty of time for the evaluation and future planning during the Caring Time. You will need to be prepared to lead this important discussion.**

To get started, take a few minutes to affirm one another with the following fun ice-breaker.

# Ice-Breaker / 15 Minutes

**Wild Predictions.** Try to match the people in your group to the wild and crazy forecasts below. (Don't take it too seriously; it's meant to be fun!) Which of the following would you choose for each of the members of your group? After you have read through the list and jotted down people's names in silence, ask one person to read the first item and everyone call out the name of the person they selected. Then move on to the next item, etc.

THE PERSON IN OUR GROUP MOST LIKELY TO ...

_____ be the first woman to win the Indianapolis 500

_____ make a million selling Beanie Babies over the Internet

_____ become famous for designing new attire for Sumo wrestlers

_____ appear on *The Tonight Show* to exhibit an acrobatic talent

_____ discover a new use for underarm deodorant

_____ move to a desert island

_____ replace Vanna White on the *Wheel of Fortune*

_____ appear on the cover of *Muscle & Fitness Magazine*

_____ write a best-selling novel based on their love life

_____ succeed David Letterman as host of *The Late Show*

_____ substitute for John Madden as Fox's football color analyst

_____ become the newest member of the Spice Girls

_____ win a blue ribbon at the state fair for Rocky Mountain oysters

_____ be a dance instructor on a cruise ship for wealthy, well-endowed widows

_____ work as a bodyguard for Rush Limbaugh at a feminist convention

_____ land a job as head librarian for Amazon.com

_____ open the Clouseau Private Detective Agency

# Bible Study / 30 Minutes

## Option 1 / Gospel Study

### Mark 3:20–21,31–35 / All in the Family

The Gospel of Mark presents Jesus as being under a lot of pressure from the crowd once they discovered he could heal them. Their demands made it so difficult for him to have time to himself that Jesus' mother and siblings felt the need to rescue him. Read Mark 3:20–21,31–35 and discuss your responses to the following questions with your group.

*²⁰Then Jesus entered a house, and again a crowd gathered, so that he and his disciples were not even able to eat. ²¹When his family heard about this, they went to take charge of him, for they said, "He is out of his mind." ...*

*³¹Then Jesus' mother and brothers arrived. Standing outside, they sent someone in to call him. ³²A crowd was sitting around him, and they told him, "Your mother and brothers are outside looking for you."*

*³³"Who are my mother and my brothers?" he asked.*

*³⁴Then he looked at those seated in a circle around him and said, "Here are my mother and my brothers! ³⁵Whoever does God's will is my brother and sister and mother."*

*1.* Have you ever experienced a conflict between what God wanted for you and what your family expected of you? What happened?

*2.* Why did Jesus' family want to "take charge of him"?
- ❏ They feared that he would overwork himself.
- ❏ They thought he had "delusions of grandeur."
- ❏ He was embarrassing them.
- ❏ They wanted to teach him proper behavior.

*3.* What would you have done if you had been a member of Jesus' family?
- ❏ I'd have gone into the house and confronted him.
- ❏ I'd have spoken to Jesus privately.
- ❏ I'd have been too embarrassed to do anything.
- ❏ I'd have ordered him to go home and be quiet.
- ❏ Nothing—I wouldn't have wanted to make a scene.

**4.** In referring to the crowd, why did Jesus answer by saying, "Here are my mother and my brothers"?
❏ He believed he belonged to the family of all humanity.
❏ He was redefining the "family of God."
❏ He placed more importance on his spiritual family than on his natural family.
❏ He was teaching the crowd that they could belong to the family of God.

**5.** How do you feel about the family you have (either the family you grew up in, or the one you are raising now)?
❏ I love each and every one of them.
❏ I don't know how I kept my sanity, but I did.
❏ I've felt torn between what God wanted and what my family wanted.
❏ Ours was/is a household of pain.
❏ Our family life was/is full of tension.
❏ I (My kids) grew up feeling secure in my (their) parents' love.
❏ I grew up feeling insecure, and searched for others to accept me.
❏ other:_____

**6.** According to these verses, what is necessary for you to become a member of the family of God?
❏ You must turn your back on your natural family.
❏ You must know and follow the will of God.
❏ You must believe that Jesus is the Son of God.
❏ You must be adopted by Jesus.

**7.** Which two of the following statements best describe your relationship with the family of God?
❏ I consider myself to be a "black sheep" in the family.
❏ I have been in the family for a long time.
❏ I'm just a baby in the family.
❏ I'm really on the outside looking in.
❏ I generally don't get along with other family members.
❏ I love all my relatives.
❏ I love most of my relatives.
❏ I've got a lot to learn about this family.
❏ I want to spend more time with my Father.

**8.** How can you improve the way you relate to your "brothers and sisters" in the family of God?

**9.** What role can parents take in helping their children to be part of the larger family of God?

❐ They should not try to protect children from the challenges God sets before them.

❐ They should always affirm other members of the family of God, even if their background (e.g., race or culture) is different.

❐ They should realize that children at some point need to separate from the control of earthly parents, but not from our heavenly Parent.

❐ They should be faithful in teaching them God's will.

❐ other:_____

COMMENT This is the first time we hear about Jesus' family. And they make quite an entrance! Jesus' family is concerned about him. What was causing his strange behavior? They aren't sure what is happening to him. Maybe he isn't able to care for himself. In addition, his message of God's kingdom was causing quite a stir everywhere. It was quite understandable that the opposition Jesus faced from the religious leaders concerned his family as well.

The family traveled about 30 miles from Nazareth to Capernaum. Their plan was set: they would take him back home with them—forcibly if they had to. After hearing Jesus, his family decides that he really must be out of his mind. Perhaps they suspected some sort of ecstatic, religiously induced mental illness. Jesus is surrounded by a crowd, so they don't want to confront him publicly. They send someone in to ask him to come out. Told that his family is outside, Jesus asks a rhetorical question, but nonetheless it causes more concern for the family.

Jesus provides a new definition of family. His family is not one of heredity, but of the Spirit of God. Neither the crowds nor his family understand what he is saying. However, his family will eventually move from doubt to faith.

## Option 2 / Epistle Study

## Ephesians 2:11–22 / Forever Family

Paul, whose primary ministry was to bring Gentiles (non-Jews) to Christ, here affirms how they have become full members of God's family. Read Ephesians 2:11–22 and discuss your responses to the following questions with your group.

*"Therefore, remember that formerly you who are Gentiles by birth and called "uncircumcised" by those who call themselves "the circumcision"*

*(that done in the body by the hands of men)—*<sup>12</sup>*remember that at that time you were separate from Christ, excluded from citizenship in Israel and foreigners to the covenants of the promise, without hope and without God in the world.* <sup>13</sup>*But now in Christ Jesus you who once were far away have been brought near through the blood of Christ.*

<sup>14</sup>*For he himself is our peace, who has made the two one and has destroyed the barrier, the dividing wall of hostility,* <sup>15</sup>*by abolishing in his flesh the law with its commandments and regulations. His purpose was to create in himself one new man out of the two, thus making peace,* <sup>16</sup>*and in this one body to reconcile both of them to God through the cross, by which he put to death their hostility.* <sup>17</sup>*He came and preached peace to you who were far away and peace to those who were near.* <sup>18</sup>*For through him we both have access to the Father by one Spirit.*

<sup>19</sup>*Consequently, you are no longer foreigners and aliens, but fellow citizens with God's people and members of God's household,* <sup>20</sup>*built on the foundation of the apostles and prophets, with Christ Jesus himself as the chief cornerstone.* <sup>21</sup>*In him the whole building is joined together and rises to become a holy temple in the Lord.* <sup>22</sup>*And in him you too are being built together to become a dwelling in which God lives by his Spirit.*

1. In high school and/or college, which groups (clubs, activities, sororities, fraternities, honor societies, informal cliques, etc.) were you not a part of but wished you were? How did you feel, being on the outside looking in?

2. Previously, why were Gentiles excluded from the family of God?

3. How did Christ make it possible for Gentiles to be included in the family of God?

4. What is the message of peace which Christ has brought to us?

5. How does one become a member of God's household? Do you consider yourself a member in good standing?

6. What are some of the benefits and privileges of being a member of the family of God?

7. How has God's Spirit been at work in your life and the life of your family?

**8.** As a parent, what "dividing wall" would you like to break down (with Christ's help)?

❒ family tensions
❒ school or neighborhood tensions
❒ racial attitudes
❒ other:_____

 # Caring Time / 15–45 Minutes

EVALUATION **1.** Take some time to evaluate the life of your group by using the statements below. Read the first sentence out loud and ask everyone to explain where they would put a dot between the two extremes. When you are finished, go back and give your group an overall grade in the categories of Group Building, Bible Study and Mission.

### ◇ GROUP BUILDING

On celebrating life and having fun together, we were more like a ...
**wet blanket** _____**hot tub**

On becoming a caring community, we were more like a ...
**prickly porcupine** _____**cuddly teddy bear**

### 📖 BIBLE STUDY

On sharing our spiritual stories, we were more like a ...
**shallow pond** _____**spring-fed lake**

On digging into Scripture, we were more like a ...
**slow-moving snail** _____**voracious anteater**

### ○→○ MISSION

On inviting new people into our group, we were more like a ...
**barbed-wire fence** _____**wide-open door**

On stretching our vision for mission, we were more like an ...
**ostrich** _____**eagle**

**2.** What are some specific areas in which you have grown in this course about family?

❒ appreciating our past and learning from the hard times

❒ handling pressures and making our family a top priority

❒ understanding each other and constructively handling our differences and conflicts

❒ including and balancing both love and discipline in parenting

❒ becoming aware of family expectations, their influence and the need for healthy expectations

❒ affirming regularly our commitment to each other

❒ other:_____

**MAKE A COVENANT**

A covenant is a promise made to each other in the presence of God. Its purpose is to indicate your intention to make yourselves available to one another for the fulfillment of the purposes you share in common. If your group is going to continue, in a spirit of prayer work your way through the following sentences, trying to reach an agreement on each statement pertaining to your ongoing life together. Write out your covenant like a contract, stating your purpose, goals and the ground rules for your group.

**1.** The purpose of our group will be:

**2.** Our goals will be:

**3.** We will meet for _____weeks, after which we will decide if we wish to continue as a group.

**4.** We will meet from _____ to _____ and we will strive to start on time and end on time.

**5.** We will meet at _____ (place) or we will rotate from house to house.

**6.** We will agree to the following ground rules for our group (check):

❒ PRIORITY: While you are in the course, you give the group meetings priority.

❒ PARTICIPATION: Everyone participates and no one dominates.

❒ RESPECT: Everyone is given the right to their own opinion, and all questions are encouraged and respected.

❑ CONFIDENTIALITY: Anything that is said in the meeting is never repeated outside the meeting.

❑ EMPTY CHAIR: The group stays open to new people at every meeting, as long as they understand the ground rules.

❑ SUPPORT: Permission is given to call upon each other in time of need at any time.

❑ ACCOUNTABILITY: We agree to let the members of the group hold us accountable to the commitments which each of us make in whatever loving ways we decide upon.

❑ MISSION: We will do everything in our power to start a new group.

# Reference Notes

**Summary.** Paul moves from the problem of human alienation from God (Eph. 2:1–10) to the related problem of alienation between people themselves (Eph. 2:11–22). In both cases, the problem is hostility (or enmity). In both cases, Christ is the one who, through his death, brings peace— first between God and people, but then, also, between human enemies. The particular focus of this passage is on the deep hostility between Jew and Gentile. Paul begins by reminding the Gentiles of their five-fold alienation from God's plan for the world (vv. 11–12). But he then goes on to describe how Jesus' death overcame all that (vv. 13–18). Jesus abolished the Law which divided (people from God, Jew from Gentile); he created a new humanity; and he reconciled this new "race" to God. Paul concludes by describing, through three metaphors (kingdom, family, temple), the new reality which has emerged (vv. 19–22).

**2:11 *remember.*** In Ephesians 2:1–3, Paul reminded his Gentile readers that once they were trapped in their transgressions and sins, and so were spiritually dead and alienated from God. Here in verse 11, he asks them to remember that once they were also isolated from all the blessings of God. In 2:1–3, the focus is on being cut off from God himself; while in verses 11–13 the focus is on being cut off from God's kingdom and God's people.

***formerly.*** The focus in verses 11–12 is on what the Gentiles once were, prior to the beginning of their spiritual quest.

**"uncircumcised."** This is a derogatory slur by which Gentiles were mocked. With this contemptuous nickname, Jews were saying that the Gentiles "lack of God's mark" on their bodies put them absolutely outside of God's kingdom, so they were to be despised.

**"the circumcision."** This is how Jews thought of themselves and was a term used with pride. Circumcision was the sign given to Abraham by which the covenant people were to be marked. This made the Jew different and special.

**2:12** Paul describes the five disabilities faced by the Gentile world prior to Christ. They were "Christless, stateless, friendless, hopeless and Godless" (Hendriksen).

**separate from Christ.** The Gentiles had no hope of a coming Messiah who would make all things right. Instead, they considered themselves to be caught up in the deadly cycle of history which led nowhere. This separation from the hope of a Messiah was the first liability faced by Gentiles.

**excluded from citizenship.** Gentiles were not part of God's kingdom. Israel was a nation founded by God, consisting of his people, and Gentiles were outside that reality. This was their second liability.

**foreigners to the covenants.** Not only did Gentiles have no part in God's kingdom, they also stood outside all the amazing agreements (covenants) God made with his people (see for example Ex. 6:6–8; Deut. 28:9–14). This is the third liability.

**without hope.** During this particular historical era, the Roman world experienced a profound loss of hope. The first century was inundated with mystery cults, all promising salvation from this despair. Living in fear of demons, people felt themselves to be mere playthings of the capricious gods. This lack of hope in the face of fear was the fourth liability.

**without God.** This is not to say that Gentiles were atheists (even though the word used here is *atheos*). On the contrary, they worshiped scores of deities. The problem was that they had no effective knowledge of the one true God. This is the final liability.

**2:13 But now.** This is the second great "But," which signals God's intervention into a seemingly hopeless situation. The first use of "But" in this fashion is found in Ephesians 2:4, where Paul describes what God has done in the face of universal sin and bondage.

**through the blood of Christ.** Paul pinpoints how this great change occurred. It is as a result of Jesus' death on the cross that union with Christ is possible (see Eph. 1:7).

**2:14 *our peace.*** Jesus brings peace; that is, he creates harmony between human beings and God. He also creates harmony between human beings. He draws together those who consider each other to be enemies. He does this by being the one who stands between the alienated parties, bridging the gap that separates them.

***the dividing wall.*** Paul has in mind an actual wall which existed in the temple in Jerusalem. The temple itself was built on an elevated area. The inner sanctuary was surrounded by the Court of the Priests. Beyond this was the Court of Israel (for men only) and then the Court of the Women. All these courts were on the same level as the temple; and each had a different degree of exclusivity. Ringing all the courts and some 19 steps below was the Court of the Gentiles. Here the Gentiles could gaze up at the temple. But they could not approach it. They were cut off by a stone wall ("the dividing wall") bearing signs that warned in Greek and Latin that trespassing foreigners would be killed. Paul himself knew well this prohibition. He had nearly been lynched by a mob of Jews who were told he had taken a Gentile into the temple.

***hostility.*** The ancient world abounded in hostility. There was enmity between Jew and Gentile, Greek and barbarian, men and women, slave and free. Christ ends each form of hostility.

**2:15–16** By means of three key verbs ("abolish," "create," and "reconcile"), Paul describes the three accomplishments of Christ on the cross whereby he destroys the "dividing wall of hostility."

**2:15 *the law with its commandments and regulations.*** The primary reference is to the thousands of rules and regulations which were in existence at the time of Christ by which Jewish leaders sought to define the "Law of Moses" (the first five books of the Old Testament). The belief was that only by keeping all these rules could one be counted "good," and therefore have fellowship with God.

***one new man.*** In the place of divided humanity, Jesus creates a whole new quality of being—a new humanity, as it were. This does not mean that Jews became Gentiles, nor that Gentiles became Jews. Both became Christians, "the third race."

**2:16 *reconcile.*** This word means "to bring together estranged parties." In verse 14 the emphasis is on reconciling Jew to Gentile. Here the reference is to bringing both Jew and Gentile together with God.

**2:17 *He came and preached peace.*** Since such peace was possible only through the Cross, this reference is probably to Jesus' post-resurrection appearances. His first words to the stunned apostles after his resurrection were, in fact, "Peace be with you" (John 20:19).

**2:18 *access.*** In Greek, one form of this word is used to describe an individual whose job it is to usher a person into the presence of the king. Indeed, not only did Jesus open the way back to God (by his death humanity was reconciled to God), he continues to provide the means whereby an ongoing and continuing relationship is possible.

**2:19–22** To describe the achievement of Jesus, Paul uses three images: that of God's kingdom, God's family and God's temple.

**2:19 *Consequently.*** Paul will now describe the results of this threefold work of Christ on the cross.

***foreigners.*** Nonresident aliens who were disliked by the native population and often held in suspicion.

***aliens.*** These are residents in a foreign land. They pay taxes, but have no legal standing and few rights.

***fellow citizens.*** Whereas once the Gentiles were "excluded from citizenship in Israel" (v. 12), now they are members of God's kingdom. They now "belong."

***members of God's household.*** In fact, they do not merely have a new legal status ("citizens"), their relationship is far more intimate. They have become family.

**2:20 *the foundation of the apostles and prophets.*** Since both apostles and prophets are teachers, this phrase could mean that the church rests on the teaching of both the Old Testament (prophets) and the New Testament (apostles). However, since the order is reversed, it probably means that the church rests on the teaching of the apostles and the New Testament prophets who followed them.

***cornerstone.*** That stone which rested firmly on the foundation and tied two walls together, giving each its correct alignment. The temple in Jerusalem had massive cornerstones (one was nearly 40 feet long). The image might be of Jesus holding together Jew and Gentile.

**2:21 *temple.*** The new temple is not like the old one, carved out of dead stone, beautiful but forbidding and exclusive. Rather, it is alive all over the world, inclusive of all, made up of the individuals in whom God dwells.

***joined together.*** Used by a mason to describe how two stones were prepared so that they would bond tightly together.